Watch & Listen

reflections on following Jesus through the Gospel of Mark

by Ruth J. Leamy

Illustrations by Lydia Leamy
The illustrations echo the title; they each represent something we use to watch or listen.

Table of Contents

INTRODUCTION

Day 1
Reading: Mark 1:1-20

Prayer

The mighty one, God the Lord, speaks. (Psalm 50:1a)
The Lord, the God of gods, has spoken. (BCP)

God has spoken, and we are going to watch for and listen to his message to us in the Gospel of Mark.

The beginning of the good news of Jesus Christ. (Mark 1:1)
The beginning of the gospel of Jesus Christ... (NKJV)

Mark doesn't take much time for an introduction. He jumps right in and introduces us to Jesus.

Let's take a moment to look at the names Mark uses. *Jesus* is the name his parents gave him. It carries the meanings of Savior, Rescuer, and Deliverer.

Christ is not Jesus' middle name; it is his title. It comes from a Greek word (*Christos)* meaning "the anointed one" or "the chosen one." It is equivalent to the Hebrew title *Messiah.*[1]

Right here, at the beginning, Mark tells his readers that this human named Jesus is also the Messiah, the Longed-for One, the Rescuer.

Mark says that Jesus Christ has brought us good news, or "the gospel." The initial audience of this book would have been familiar with the term "gospel" (*euaggelizo*). The Romans employed this term to describe their festivities honoring the emperor they revered. It was a word that celebrated a new beginning and "a radically new situation to the world."[2]

Mark's opening sentence immediately grabs my attention. Of course, I want to hear about this Rescuer and Deliverer! And the possibility of a radically new world–tell me more!

As it is written in the prophet Isaiah, "See, I am sending my messenger ahead of you, who will prepare your way, the voice of one crying out in the wilderness: 'Prepare the way of the Lord; make his paths straight,' " so John the baptizer appeared in the wilderness, proclaiming a baptism of repentance for the forgiveness of sins. And the whole Judean region and all the people of Jerusalem were going out to him and were baptized by him in the River Jordan, confessing their sins. Now John was clothed with camel's hair, with a leather belt around his waist, and he ate locusts and wild honey. He proclaimed, "The one who is more powerful than I is coming after me; I am not worthy to stoop down and untie the strap of his sandals. I have baptized you with water, but he will baptize you with the Holy Spirit." (Mark 2:1-8)

Mark introduces us to John the Baptist, a messenger sent by God to "prepare the way of the Lord." John proclaimed that a powerful one was coming.

In those days Jesus came from Nazareth of Galilee and was baptized by John in the Jordan. And just as he was coming up out of the water, he saw the heavens torn apart and the Spirit descending like a dove upon him. And a voice came from the heavens, "You are my Son, the Beloved; with you I am well pleased.

And the Spirit immediately drove him out into the wilderness. He was in the wilderness forty days, tested by

Satan, and he was with the wild beasts, and the angels waited on him. (Mark 1:9-13)

Mark briefly summarizes Jesus' baptism and his temptation in the wilderness. He includes God the Father's own introduction of Jesus: "My Son, the Beloved; with you I am well pleased."

After this whirlwind of introductions and events, we hear Jesus' own words for the first time in this Gospel:

Now after John was arrested, Jesus came to Galilee proclaiming the good news of God and saying, "The time is fulfilled, and the kingdom of God has come near; repent, and believe in the good news." (Mark 1:14-15)

The word Jesus used for time (*kairos*) refers not so much to a specific moment but to a "supreme moment."[3] This is Jesus' call to each of us to come near to him, to repent, and to believe in the good news.

Let's ponder the word *repent* for a minute. In Greek, the word is *metanoeo*, which means to think differently, to reconsider,[4] or "to change our perception."[5] Repentance is more than regret; it is different from guilt; it is an intentional change and a choice to walk in a new direction. Repentance is possible because God has come near to us. He is with us and within us, pulling us out of the ruts we have become bogged down in, awakening us from indifference. Repentance is not a self-help program. It is a change of heart enabled by God.

Next, Mark shows us Jesus calling others to follow him and share this good news:

As Jesus passed along the Sea of Galilee, he saw Simon and his brother Andrew casting a net into the sea, for they were fishers. And Jesus said to them, "Follow me, and I will make you fishers of people." And immediately they left their nets and followed him.

As he went a little farther, he saw James son of Zebedee

and his brother John, who were in their boat mending the nets. Immediately he called them, and they left their father Zebedee in the boat with the hired men and followed him. (Mark 1:16-20)

According to the other Gospel books, this was not the first time Jesus met these men. But although they were acquainted with him, they certainly had no idea where their journey of following him would lead.

The first disciple that Mark mentions is Simon, soon to be renamed Peter. Mark had a close relationship with Peter. In fact, Peter eventually considered Mark to be his spiritual son. [6]

Meet the Author

Mark, also known as John Mark, is mentioned in the book of Acts. He was the son of a wealthy woman named Mary, who allowed the early church to meet in her home (possibly the same place where Jesus and his disciples celebrated the Last Supper). In the book of Acts, we see the Apostle Peter seeking refuge at Mary's house after escaping from prison.

Mark had an uncle named Barnabas, who was described as an encourager. When Barnabas traveled with the Apostle Paul to spread the gospel, Mark joined them. However, during one of these journeys, Mark left the team. The Scriptures don't provide many details, but this event led to a serious disagreement between Paul and Barnabas. Paul found a new preaching partner (Silas), while Barnabas took Mark and went to Cyprus.

This time with Barnabas the Encourager must have been

effective because the next thing we hear about Mark is Paul describing him as "a comfort to me" and "helpful to me in my ministry."[7]

According to church historians, Mark ministered with the Apostle Peter in Rome, and he collected Peter's memories of his time watching and listening to Jesus into the Gospel book we are now studying. Mark was instrumental in planting several churches, and his life ended in martyrdom.

Putting together all these details, we can see that Mark was acquainted with the Apostles and involved with the early church from its beginning. (He may even mention himself in the Garden of Gethsemane with Jesus—but we'll get to that later.) We can see that Mark was a man who experienced success as well as failure. He was an integral part of Paul's team—but then he split up the team. He was no stranger to the concept of repentance and letting God bring about healthy change in his life.

While reading Mark's gospel, we'll frequently see his references to the disciples' shortcomings and moments of doubt. Perhaps Mark was reminding us that, like him, and like the disciples, we are all imperfect, but Jesus loves and values us all.

Mark writes in a brief and earnest style, often using the word "immediately." His use of this word makes me think of a modern phrase: "just like that."

Mark gives us fewer words of Jesus than the other Gospel writers: that is why, in this study, we are watching as well as listening to Jesus. We aim to observe the nature of Jesus' character and how he engages with people.

I find the book of Mark to be particularly relevant during the season of Lent. Good Friday looms in the distance. Easter is on the distant horizon. The mercy and love of Jesus (as demonstrated on Good Friday) and the power of God (as revealed on Easter Morning) call me and empower me to repent:

- to change my mind to echo the loving and merciful attitude of Jesus,
- to change my direction to follow and focus on Jesus,
- and to respond to Jesus with heartfelt prayer.

Mark's often-used "immediately" urges me to jump in today, right now, to follow Jesus in everyday life activities, aware that if I fail, Jesus will forgive me and offer a new beginning.

A Journey through Mark

I divided the book of Mark into thirty-one sections, arranged in chapters or weeks of five daily readings. Each chapter begins with a verse from Psalms.[8] These verses will become simple daily prayers to begin each daily reading.

I chose to print the readings from Mark in several different translations because some readings are expressed more clearly in specific translations. (Detail-oriented people will notice that different translations have different rules of capitalization.) Of course, you can pick up your own Bible and follow along in your favorite version if you desire.

After each daily reading, I wrote a brief observation summarizing the points that intrigued or inspired me. They're not extensive theological essays, just my own insights that I trust you might also find relevant. I pray that these remarks may prompt your own unique observations.

Each daily segment ends with a prayer which is my personal response to the Scripture passage. I have inserted lined pages throughout the book so you have plenty of room to write your prayers and thoughts as we journey together, watching and listening to Jesus.

Ponder

Review page 4 and 5 for the definitions of *Jesus*, *Christ*, and *Gospel.* Which one of these catches your attention today?

Look back at the first quote from Jesus that Mark gives us (page 6, Mark 1:14–15). Why is the theme of repentance such good news?

Respond

Speak to me, Lord,
as I read your word.
Open my eyes to see you at work
on the page and in the world.
Open my ears to hear your call
and listen to your guidance.
Tell me your Good News today.

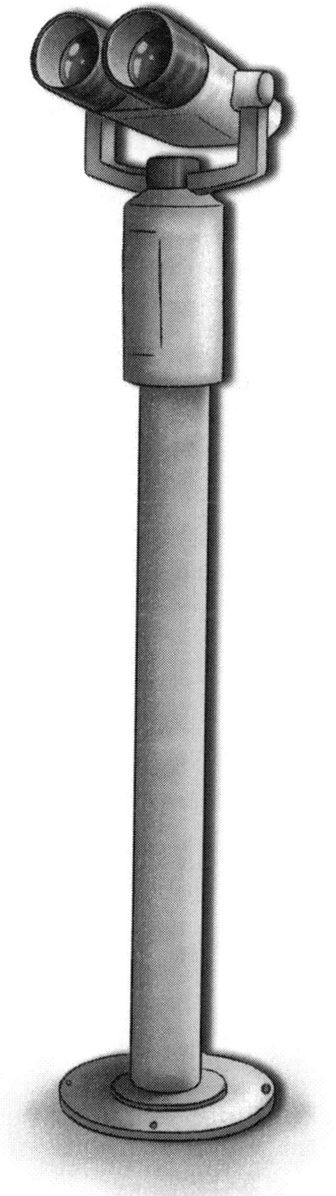

Note: In each chapter, you will find one reading with this viewfinder graphic. These readings are the ones I suggest focusing on in a group discussion. (See "Using this book in a group" in the Appendix on page 143.)

WEEK 1
Watch & Listen to Jesus the Teacher

Reading: Mark 1:21-45, Mark 2, & Mark 3

Prayer

Make me to know your ways, O Lord;
teach me your paths. (Psalm 25:4)
Let me know Your ways, O Lord;
Teach me Your paths. (AMP)
Show me how you work, God;
School me in your ways. (MSG)
Show me the right path, O Lord;
point out the road for me to follow. (NLT)
Show me your ways, O Lord,
and teach me your paths. (BCP)

Day 2: Mark 1:21-45

Make me to know your ways, O Lord;
teach me your paths. (Psalm 25:4)

They went to Capernaum, and when the Sabbath came, he entered the synagogue and taught. They were astounded at his teaching, for he taught them as one having authority and not as the scribes.

Just then there was in their synagogue a man with an unclean spirit, and he cried out, "What have you to do with us, Jesus of Nazareth? Have you come to destroy us? I know who you are, the Holy One of God."

But Jesus rebuked him, saying, "Be quiet and come out of him!" And the unclean spirit, convulsing him and crying with a loud voice, came out of him.

They were all amazed, and they kept on asking one another, "What is this? A new teaching—with authority! He commands even the unclean spirits, and they obey him." At once his fame began to spread throughout the surrounding region of Galilee.

As soon as they left the synagogue, they entered the house of Simon and Andrew, with James and John. Now Simon's mother-in-law was in bed with a fever, and they told him about her at once. He came and took her by the hand and lifted her up. Then the fever left her, and she began to serve them.

That evening, at sunset, they brought to him all who were sick or possessed by demons. And the whole city was gathered around the door. And he cured many who were sick with various diseases and cast out many demons, and he would not permit the demons to speak, because they knew him.

In the morning, while it was still very dark, he got up and went out to a deserted place, and there he prayed. And Simon and his companions hunted for him. When they found him, they said to him, "Everyone is searching for you."

He answered, "Let us go on to the neighboring towns, so that I may proclaim the message there also, for that is what I came out to do." And he went throughout all Galilee, proclaiming the message in their synagogues and casting out demons.

A man with a skin disease came to him begging him, and kneeling he said to him, "If you are willing, you can make me clean."

Moved with pity, Jesus stretched out his hand and touched him and said to him, "I am willing. Be made clean!" Immediately the skin disease left him, and he was made clean. After sternly warning him he sent him away at once, saying to him, "See that you say nothing to anyone, but go, show yourself to the priest, and offer for your cleansing what Moses commanded as a testimony to them." But he went out and began to proclaim it freely and to spread the word, so that Jesus could no longer go into a town openly but stayed out in the country, and people came to him from every quarter.

Define

He taught them as one having authority and not as the scribes: Unlike other teachers, Jesus was not quoting other sources or explaining the teachings of others. He taught his own new message.[1]

Observe

Good teachers have a natural authority that makes us recognize their trustworthiness. In today's reading, I see Jesus demonstrate his authority over

- illness in general
- terrifying diseases such as leprosy
- conditions caused by forces beyond my understanding

Essential elements of teaching include a plan and a schedule. Over and over, we will hear Jesus telling those he healed not to talk about their miracle. Jesus knew that his time on earth was limited, and he needed to focus on teaching without being inundated by individuals solely seeking miracles rather than listening to his message.

Teachers must also seek guidance and nourishment for themselves. Mark showed us Jesus carving out time to be with his Father.

Ponder

Look back at the list above of things that Jesus has authority over. What would you add to the list?

How does Jesus' authority give you comfort?

Respond

Dear Jesus my Teacher,

Help me to listen to your voice of authority

which can liberate me from unhealthy habits

and empower me to walk your path of love and faithfulness.

Teach me your ways, O Lord,
that I may live according to your truth!
(Psalm 86:11 NLT)

Day 3: Mark 2:1-17

Make me to know your ways, O Lord;
teach me your paths. (Psalm 25:4)

When Jesus returned to Capernaum several days later, the news spread quickly that he was back home. Soon the house where he was staying was so packed with visitors that there was no more room, even outside the door. While he was preaching God's word to them, four men arrived carrying a paralyzed man on a mat. They couldn't bring him to Jesus because of the crowd, so they dug a hole through the roof above his head. Then they lowered the man on his mat, right down in front of Jesus. Seeing their faith, Jesus said to the paralyzed man, "My child, your sins are forgiven."

But some of the teachers of religious law who were sitting there thought to themselves, "What is he saying? This is blasphemy! Only God can forgive sins!"

Jesus knew immediately what they were thinking, so he asked them, "Why do you question this in your hearts? Is it easier to say to the paralyzed man 'Your sins are forgiven,' or 'Stand up, pick up your mat, and walk'? So I will prove to you that the Son of Man has the authority on earth to forgive sins." Then Jesus turned to the paralyzed man and said, "Stand up, pick up your mat, and go home!"

And the man jumped up, grabbed his mat, and walked out through the stunned onlookers. They were all amazed and praised God, exclaiming, "We've never seen anything like this before!"

Then Jesus went out to the lakeshore again and taught the crowds that were coming to him. As he walked along, he saw Levi son of Alphaeus sitting at his tax collector's booth. "Follow me and be my disciple," Jesus said to him. So Levi got up and followed him.

Later, Levi invited Jesus and his disciples to his home as dinner guests, along with many tax collectors and other disreputable sinners. (There were many people of this kind among Jesus' followers.) But when the teachers of religious law who were Pharisees saw him eating with tax collectors and other sinners, they asked his disciples, "Why does he eat with such scum?"

When Jesus heard this, he told them, "Healthy people don't need a doctor—sick people do. I have come to call not those who think they are righteous, but those who know they are sinners." (Mark 2:1-17 NLT)

Define

the house where he was staying: In Mark 1:29, Jesus lodged at the home of Simon Peter while he was in Capernaum. It is likely that Jesus continued to stay with Peter each time he visited the city. The text refers to him being "back home."

tax collector: This was not simply a choice of employment. As agents of the merciless government of Rome, tax collectors were viewed as traitors–people to be hated and shunned.

Levi's dinner guests: If respectable people viewed Levi as a traitor to be shunned, it is not difficult to see why his only friends were "disreputable sinners."

Observe

This passage demonstrated several unique ways that people met Jesus. The disabled man was utterly dependent on his friends to carry him to Jesus (which they did with great determination). Levi (soon to be renamed Matthew) was in the middle of his workday when Jesus approached him. Levi's friends met Jesus at a party. These varied experiences assure me that Jesus is reaching out to all of us personally and uniquely.

I have always wondered how the owner of the house reacted when a hole suddenly appeared in his ceiling. I was fascinated to learn this was probably Peter's house. Peter seems like the kind of person who might rush up to the roof and help the men give their friend access to Jesus.

Ponder

Which of the characters in this reading do you most wish you could meet?

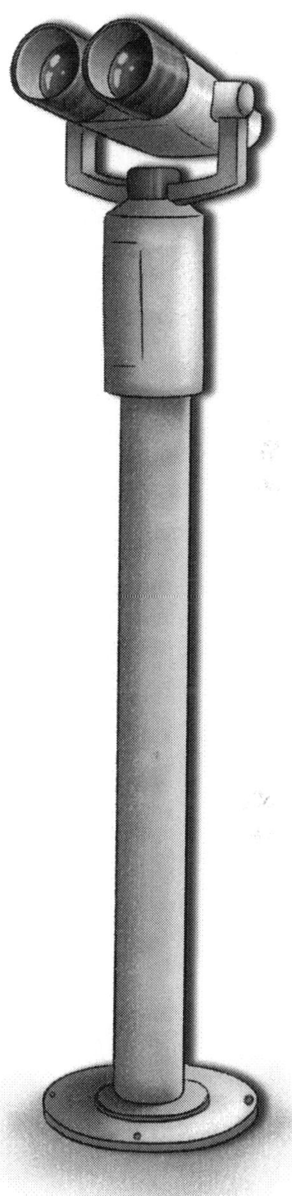

What did today's Scripture reading tell you about Jesus' character and attitude?

What did today's Scriptures tell you about how Jesus interacts with people?

How would you summarize Jesus' message in this reading, considering his actions and his words?

You will notice that one weekly reading has more questions to ponder than the others. This is the reading to focus on in a weekly group discussion. (See page 143.)

Respond

Jesus, my Teacher,
I am deeply conscious of the fact
that I need you.
I need your teaching to guide my decisions.
I need your healing touch
when I feel helpless.
And I need your power and authority
to change my life.

> *Look upon me with love;*
> *teach me your decrees.*
> *(Psalm 119:135 NLT)*

Day 4: Mark 2:18-3:6

Make me to know your ways, O Lord;
teach me your paths. (Psalm 25:4)

The disciples of John and the disciples of the Pharisees made a practice of fasting. Some people confronted Jesus: "Why do the followers of John and the Pharisees take on the discipline of fasting, but your followers don't?"

Jesus said, "When you're celebrating a wedding, you don't skimp on the cake and wine. You feast. Later you may need to pull in your belt, but not now. As long as the bride and groom are with you, you have a good time. No one throws cold water on a friendly bonfire. This is Kingdom Come!"

He went on, "No one cuts up a fine silk scarf to patch old work clothes; you want fabrics that match. And you don't put your wine in cracked bottles."

One Sabbath day he was walking through a field of ripe grain. As his disciples made a path, they pulled off heads of grain. The Pharisees told on them to Jesus: "Look, your disciples are breaking Sabbath rules!"

Jesus said, "Really? Haven't you ever read what David did when he was hungry, along with those who were with him? How he entered the sanctuary and ate fresh bread off the altar, with the Chief Priest Abiathar right there watching—holy bread that no one but priests were allowed to eat—and handed it out to his companions?" Then Jesus said, "The Sabbath was made to serve us; we weren't made to serve the Sabbath. The Son of Man is no yes-man to the Sabbath. He's in charge!"

Then he went back in the meeting place where he found a man with a crippled hand. The Pharisees had their eyes on Jesus to see if he would heal him, hoping to catch him in a Sabbath violation. He said to the man with the crippled hand, "Stand here where we can see you."

Then he spoke to the people: "What kind of action suits the Sabbath best? Doing good or doing evil? Helping people or leaving them helpless?" No one said a word. He looked them in the eye, one after another, angry now, furious at their hard-nosed religion. He said to the man, "Hold out your hand." He held it out—it was as good as new! The Pharisees got out as fast as they could, sputtering about how they would join forces with Herod's followers and ruin him. (Mark 2:18-3:6 MSG)

Define

Herod's followers: There were quite a few kings named Herod, and none were known for doing good. Bible scholars are not sure whether the people mentioned here are a political or religious group. What is intriguing is that diverse groups were forming alliances against Jesus – groups that typically did not collaborate. People in positions of authority were beginning to see him as a threat.

Observe

In today's Scriptures, religious leaders criticized Jesus and his followers for not following their extensive list of rules and traditions, including a regular practice of fasting.

Fasting is meant to draw us closer to God. We choose to put something aside for a time to focus more clearly on God. Jesus said the disciples did not need to do this while he was physically present with them.

The motives of the religious leaders became clear when Jesus healed a man on the Sabbath. Far from being interested in the health and well-being of their congregation, they were focused only on retaining their own power.

Within the reading, Jesus hinted that his disciples would find reasons to fast in the future. In the book of Acts, the early church members used fasting as a prayer practice.

Fasting can be a spiritual exercise, a way to strengthen our powers of self-control. Choosing to fast from food in general or from some types of foods or activities is a very personal choice–something to discuss with the Lord before jumping into a commitment.

Fasting can be meaningful and beneficial. However, it can also lead to a sense of pride, whether we openly discuss our fasting commitments or take pride in abstaining from fasting because we perceive it as futile. It is important to remember that we cannot see the motives and the inner attitudes of others.

Ponder

What is your experience with fasting? Have you seen it used as a helpful spiritual discipline or as a matter of pride?

Have you ever felt called by God to fast?

Respond

Deliver me, Teaching Lord,
from worshiping at the altar of What Will People Think.
Reveal to me the traditions and religious practices
that will draw me closer to you.
Revive my heart to find new meaning and relevance
in any of my practices that may have grown stale.
Show me if there are habits that have become distractions to me.
Set me free from criticizing others who may find different practices
that lead them into closer fellowship with you.

> *Teach me to do your will, for you are my God.*
> *May your gracious Spirit lead me forward on a firm footing.*
> *(Psalm 143:10 NLT)*

Day 5: Mark 3:7-19

Make me to know your ways, O Lord;
teach me your paths. (Psalm 25:4)

Jesus withdrew to the sea with His disciples; and a large crowd from Galilee followed Him; and also people from Judea, and from Jerusalem, and from Idumea, and [from the region] beyond the Jordan, and around Tyre and Sidon; a vast number of people came to Him because they were hearing about all [the things] that He was doing. And He told His disciples to have a small boat stand ready for Him because of the many people, so that they would not crowd Him; for He had healed many, and as a result all who had diseases pressed around Him to touch Him. Whenever the unclean spirits saw Him, they fell down before Him and screamed out, "You are the Son of God!" Jesus sternly warned them [again and again] not to tell who He was.

He went up on the hillside and called those whom He Himself wanted and chose; and they came to Him. And He appointed twelve [disciples], so that they would be with Him [for instruction] and so that He could send them out to preach [the gospel as apostles—that is, as His special messengers, personally chosen representatives], and to have authority and power to cast out demons. He appointed the twelve: Simon (to whom He gave the name Peter), and James, the son of Zebedee, and John the brother of James (to them He gave the name Boanerges, that is, "Sons of Thunder"); and [He also appointed] Andrew, and Philip, and Bartholomew (Nathanael), and Matthew (Levi the tax collector), and Thomas, and James the son of Alphaeus, and Thaddaeus (Judas the son of James), and Simon the Zealot; and Judas Iscariot, who betrayed Him. (Mark 3:7-19 AMP)

Observe

After teaching and ministering to a multitude, Jesus chose twelve men to become his inner circle. He had called these men to follow him earlier in his ministry, but now he made it official.

What did they think and expect now? Did they wonder if Jesus might be their longed-for Messiah? Were they hoping for positions of power and prestige as his close friends? Were they simply thinking it was a great privilege to be chosen by the up-and-coming Rabbi?

Throughout the years of Jesus' ministry, the disciples seemed to be continually competing for power. Jesus often spoke to them about how to become great in his kingdom:

> *He sat down, called the twelve, and said to them, "Whoever wants to be first must be last of all and servant of all." (Mark 9:35)*
> *...Whoever wishes to become great among you must be your servant. (Mark 10:43)*

Ponder

What do you think you would have enjoyed about being a disciple? What would you have found challenging?

Respond

Teaching Savior,

I see that you called your followers to do more than listen to your words,

and to do more than just observe your way of living.

You called them to speak your message

and to live as you lived.

Show me today how I can humbly put your instructions into practice.

> *He leads the humble in what is right*
> *and teaches the humble his way.*
> *(Psalm 25:9)*

Day 6: Mark 3:20-35

***Make me to know your ways, O Lord;
teach me your paths. (Psalm 25:4)***

Jesus came home and, as usual, a crowd gathered—so many making demands on him that there wasn't even time to eat. His friends heard what was going on and went to rescue him, by force if necessary. They suspected he was believing his own press.

The religion scholars from Jerusalem came down spreading rumors that he was working black magic, using devil tricks to impress them with spiritual power. Jesus confronted their slander with a story: "Does it make sense to send a devil to catch a devil, to use Satan to get rid of Satan? A constantly squabbling family disintegrates. If Satan were fighting Satan, there soon wouldn't be any Satan left. Do you think it's possible in broad daylight to enter the house of an awake, able-bodied man, and walk off with his possessions unless you tie him up first? Tie him up, though, and you can clean him out.

"Listen to this carefully. I'm warning you. There's nothing done or said that can't be forgiven. But if you persist in your slanders against God's Holy Spirit, you are repudiating the very One who forgives, sawing off the branch on which you're sitting, severing by your own perversity all connection with the One who forgives." He gave this warning because they were accusing him of being in league with Evil.

Just then his mother and brothers showed up. Standing outside, they relayed a message that they wanted a word with him. He was surrounded by the crowd when he was given the message, "Your mother and brothers and sisters are outside looking for you."

*Jesus responded, "Who do you think are my mother and brothers?" Looking around, taking in everyone seated around him, he said, "Right here, right in front of you—my mother and my brothers. Obedience is thicker than blood. The person who obeys God's will is my brother and sister and mother."
(Mark 3:20-35 MSG)*

Observe

In this passage, Jesus came home (possibly to Peter's

house), where his family didn't understand him, and religious leaders misjudged him. It is comforting to realize that when we feel misunderstood and misjudged by those around us, Jesus understands our experience.

Jesus' family couldn't grasp all the details of his ministry and where it would eventually lead. Notice that Mark doesn't say that Jesus completely ignored his family. He shows us Jesus using a teachable moment to look at the crowd around him and tell them they mattered to him – they were as valuable to him as his family.

Ponder

Think of a Christian you admire – perhaps a hero, a saint, or a leader. Now, take a moment to realize that Jesus loves you and values you just as much as he loves and values that person.

Respond

Jesus my Teacher,
I see that the religious leaders made a grave mistake
when they looked at you
–the One that God the Father calls "Beloved"–
and they declared that you were wicked.
Lord, I know that everyone I meet
is someone you call "Beloved."
Deliver me from quick judgments,
prejudice, and hatred.

Let my cry come right into your presence, God;
provide me with the insight that comes only from your Word.
(Psalm 119:169 MSG)

WEEK 2
Watch & Listen to Jesus the Listener

Reading: Mark 4-6

Prayer

For he did not despise or abhor the affliction of the afflicted;
He did not hide his face from me,
but heard when I cried to him. (Psalm 22:24)
For He has not despised nor detested
the suffering of the afflicted;
Nor has He hidden His face from him;
But when he cried to Him for help, He listened. (AMP)
He has never let you down,
never looked the other way
when you were being kicked around.
He has never wandered off to do his own thing;
he has been right there, listening. (MSG)
For he has not ignored or belittled the suffering of the needy.
He has not turned his back on them,
but has listened to their cries for help. (NLT)
For he does not despise nor abhor the poor in their poverty;
neither does he hide his face from them;
but when they cry to him, he hears them. (BCP)

Day 7: Mark 4:1-34

He did not hide his face from me
but heard when I cried to him. (Psalm 22:24)

Again he began to teach beside the sea. Such a very large crowd gathered around him that he got into a boat on the sea and sat there, while the whole crowd was beside the sea on the land. He began to teach them many things in parables, and in his teaching he said to them: "Listen! A sower went out to sow. And as he sowed, some seed fell on a path, and the birds came and ate it up. Other seed fell on rocky ground, where it did not have much soil, and it sprang up quickly, since it had no depth of soil. And when the sun rose, it was scorched, and since it had no root it withered away. Other seed fell among thorns, and the thorns grew up and choked it, and it yielded no grain. Other seed fell into good soil and brought forth grain, growing up and increasing and yielding thirty and sixty and a hundredfold." And he said, "If you have ears to hear, then hear!"

When he was alone, those who were around him along with the twelve asked him about the parables. And he said to them, "To you has been given the secret of the kingdom of God, but for those outside everything comes in parables, in order that 'they may indeed look but not perceive, and may indeed hear but not understand; so that they may not turn again and be forgiven.' "

And he said to them, "Do you not understand this parable? Then how will you understand all the parables? The sower sows the word. These are the ones on the path where the word is sown: when they hear, Satan immediately comes and takes away the word that is sown in them. And these are the ones sown on rocky ground: when they hear the word, they immediately receive it with joy. But they have no root and endure only for a while; then, when trouble or persecution arises on account of the word, immediately they fall away. And others are those sown among the thorns: these are the ones who hear the word, but the cares of the age and the lure of wealth and the desire for other things come in and choke the word, and it yields nothing. And these are the ones sown on the good soil: they hear the word and accept it and bear fruit, thirty and sixty and a hundredfold."

He said to them, "Is a lamp brought in to be put under the bushel basket or under the bed and not on the lampstand? For there is nothing hidden, except to be disclosed; nor is anything secret, except to come to light. If you have ears to hear, then hear!" And he said to them, "Pay attention to what you hear; the measure you give will be the measure you get, and it will be added to you. For to those who have, more will be given, and from those who have nothing, even what they have will be taken away."

He also said, "The kingdom of God is as if someone would scatter seed on the ground and would sleep and rise night and day, and the seed would sprout and grow, he does not know how. The earth produces of itself first the stalk, then the head, then the full grain in the head. But when the grain is ripe, at once he goes in with his sickle because the harvest has come."

He also said, "With what can we compare the kingdom of God, or what parable will we use for it? It is like a mustard seed, which, when sown upon the ground, is the smallest of all the seeds on earth, yet when it is sown it grows up and becomes the greatest of all shrubs and puts forth large branches, so that the birds of the air can make nests in its shade."

With many such parables he spoke the word to them as they were able to hear it; he did not speak to them except in parables, but he explained everything in private to his disciples. (NRSVUE)

Define

they may indeed look but not perceive: This is a quote from Isaiah 6, which speaks of a stubborn refusal to hear spiritual truth.

Observe

Jesus often spoke in parables as he taught the crowds. In these short messages, he used familiar everyday objects to illustrate important spiritual truths. Parables, according to Bible scholar Michael Card, "demand interaction. By their very nature, they reveal the character of the person who listens (or doesn't listen) to them."[1] Parables were wonderful tools because they were easily repeatable and shareable. Listeners could take home the concepts in the stories even if they didn't remember them word for word. They could mull over them and discuss them with others as the meaning gradually dawned upon them. They would also remember the parable every time they saw the objects or situations that were mentioned in it.

Between the parables, we see Jesus hearing the disciples and being sensitive to their needs.

Ponder

Look around your home and your surroundings. What objects do you think Jesus would use today if he were sharing contemporary parables?

Respond

Lord, today I realized that you,
my teaching Savior who speaks to me,
always have time to listen to me.
And so today
I recommit to conversation:
to bring to you
not only my needs and worries
but also my gratitude
and my listening heart.

> *The Lord has heard my supplication*
> *[my plea for grace];*
> *The Lord receives my prayer.*
> *(Psalm 6:9 AMP)*

Day 8: Mark 4:35-5:20

...He did not hide his face from me
but heard when I cried to him. (Psalm 22:24)

As evening came, Jesus said to his disciples, "Let's cross to the other side of the lake." So they took Jesus in the boat and started out, leaving the crowds behind (although other boats followed). But soon a fierce storm came up. High waves were breaking into the boat, and it began to fill with water.

Jesus was sleeping at the back of the boat with his head on a cushion. The disciples woke him up, shouting, "Teacher, don't you care that we're going to drown?"

When Jesus woke up, he rebuked the wind and said to the waves, "Silence! Be still!" Suddenly the wind stopped, and there was a great calm. Then he asked them, "Why are you afraid? Do you still have no faith?"

The disciples were absolutely terrified. "Who is this man?" they asked each other. "Even the wind and waves obey him!"

So they arrived at the other side of the lake, in the region of the Gerasenes. When Jesus climbed out of the boat, a man possessed by an evil spirit came out from the tombs to meet him. This man lived in the burial caves and could no longer be restrained, even with a chain. Whenever he was put into chains and shackles—as he often was—he snapped the chains from his wrists and smashed the shackles. No one was strong enough to subdue him. Day and night he wandered among the burial caves and in the hills, howling and cutting himself with sharp stones.

When Jesus was still some distance away, the man saw him, ran to meet him, and bowed low before him. With a shriek, he screamed, "Why are you interfering with me, Jesus, Son of the Most High God? In the name of God, I beg you, don't torture me!"

For Jesus had already said to the spirit, "Come out of the man, you evil spirit." Then Jesus demanded, "What is your name?"

And he replied, "My name is Legion, because there are many of us inside this man." Then the evil spirits begged him again and again not to send them to some distant place. There happened to be a large herd of pigs feeding on the hillside nearby. "Send us into those pigs," the spirits begged. "Let us enter them."

So Jesus gave them permission. The evil spirits came out of the man and entered the pigs, and the entire herd of about 2,000 pigs plunged down the steep hillside into the lake and drowned in the water. The herdsmen fled to the nearby town and the surrounding countryside, spreading the news as they ran. People rushed out to see what had happened. A crowd soon gathered around Jesus, and they saw the man who had been possessed by the legion of demons. He was sitting there fully clothed and perfectly sane, and they were all afraid. Then those who had seen what happened told the others about the demon-possessed man and the pigs. And the crowd began pleading with Jesus to go away and leave them alone.

As Jesus was getting into the boat, the man who had been demon-possessed begged to go with him. But Jesus said, "No, go home to your family, and tell them everything the Lord has done for you and how merciful he has been." So the man started off to visit the Ten Towns of that region and began to proclaim the great things Jesus had done for him; and everyone was amazed at what he told them. (NLT)

Define

the region of the Gerasenes: This area just east of the Sea of Galilee was home to many Gentiles. This explains why there was a pig farm, which would not exist in a predominantly Jewish area.

Observe

Today we observed several vivid demonstrations of Jesus' power to change the natural world and to transform humans. It always fascinates me to read the disciples were terrified *after* Jesus calmed the storm. Who is this Rabbi they have agreed to follow?

When they all finally reached the shore, they did not have a moment to rejoice in their safety before they were met by a frightening individual who was beyond everyone's control – the terror of his town. There are a lot of puzzling details here about demons and pigs, but what catches my attention is the ending scene. The transformed man begged Jesus to let him join the disciples. Jesus listened to him but didn't grant his request. Instead, he urged the man to become his witness in his home area – an area which Jesus had just been ordered to leave.

The man must have followed Jesus' instructions and seems to have made an impact. The next time Jesus visited the region, the people knew all about him and begged him to heal a deaf man (Mark 7:31-37).

Ponder

Today we read about Jesus' power to calm forces of nature as well as out-of-control people. Take a moment to talk to Jesus about an aspect of your life that needs his calming touch.

Respond

Listening Lord,
today I see that you are
always hearing
and always delivering.
Sometimes you deliver me to a future
I do not expect.
But just because the outcome is unexpected
doesn't mean you didn't hear me.

> *Listen, God, I'm calling at the top of my lungs:*
> *"Be good to me! Answer me!"*
> *When my heart whispered, "Seek God,"*
> *my whole being replied,*
> *"I'm seeking him!" (Psalm 27:7-8 MSG)*

Day 9: Mark 5:21-43

...He did not hide his face from me
but heard when I cried to him. (Psalm 22:24)

When Jesus had again crossed over in the boat to the other side [of the sea], a large crowd gathered around Him; and so He stayed by the seashore. One of the synagogue officials named Jairus came up; and seeing Him, fell at His feet and begged anxiously with Him, saying, "My little daughter is at the point of death; [please] come and lay Your hands on her, so that she will be healed and live." And Jesus went with him; and a large crowd followed Him and pressed in around Him [from all sides].

A woman [in the crowd] had [suffered from] a hemorrhage for twelve years, and had endured much [suffering] at the hands of many physicians. She had spent all that she had and was not helped at all, but instead had become worse. She had heard [reports] about Jesus, and she came up behind Him in the crowd and touched His outer robe. For she thought, "If I just touch His clothing, I will get well." Immediately her flow of blood was dried up; and she felt in her body [and knew without any doubt] that she was healed of her suffering.

Immediately Jesus, recognizing in Himself that power had gone out from Him, turned around in the crowd and asked, "Who touched My clothes?"

His disciples said to Him, "You see the crowd pressing in around You [from all sides], and You ask, 'Who touched Me?'" Still He kept looking around to see the woman who had done it. And the woman, though she was afraid and trembling, aware of what had happened to her, came and fell down before Him and told Him the whole truth. Then He said to her, "Daughter, your faith [your personal trust and confidence in Me] has restored you to health; go in peace and be [permanently] healed from your suffering."

While He was still

speaking, some people came from the synagogue official's house, saying [to Jairus], "Your daughter has died; why bother the Teacher any longer?"

Overhearing what was being said, Jesus said to the synagogue official, "Do not be afraid; only keep on believing [in Me and my power]." And He allowed no one to go with Him [as witnesses], except Peter and James and John the brother of James. They came to the house of the synagogue official; and He looked [with understanding] at the uproar and commotion, and people loudly weeping and wailing [in mourning].

When He had gone in, He said to them, "Why make a commotion and weep? The child has not died, but is sleeping." They began laughing [scornfully] at Him [because they knew the child was dead]. But He made them all go outside, and took along the child's father and mother and His own [three] companions, and entered the room where the child was. Taking the child's hand, He said [tenderly] to her, "Talitha kum!"—which translated [from Aramaic] means, "Little girl, I say to you, get up!" The little girl immediately got up and began to walk, for she was twelve years old. And immediately they [who witnessed the child's resurrection] were overcome with great wonder and utter amazement. He gave strict orders that no one should know about this, and He told them to give her something to eat. (AMP)

Define

faith: In this passage, the Amplified version gives us a simple definition of faith as personal trust and confidence in Jesus.

Observe

Today's reading tells the stories of two women and their life-changing encounters with Jesus. One woman was young and wealthy with caring parents. The other woman had become frail and poor after years of illness. The cleanliness laws of her culture kept her isolated. The younger woman's father sought out Jesus and begged for his healing help. The other woman had no one to speak for her, so in desperation, she simply reached out to Jesus.

Although she hoped for a silent miracle, Jesus urged her to speak up and share what had just happened to her.

In the meantime, the distraught father of the young woman stood close by, filled with apprehension that it might be too late. When Jesus miraculously revived his daughter, he must have been flooded with joy and gratitude. Mark does not give us any words from the young woman. I like to imagine that she shared her story whenever she had the chance.

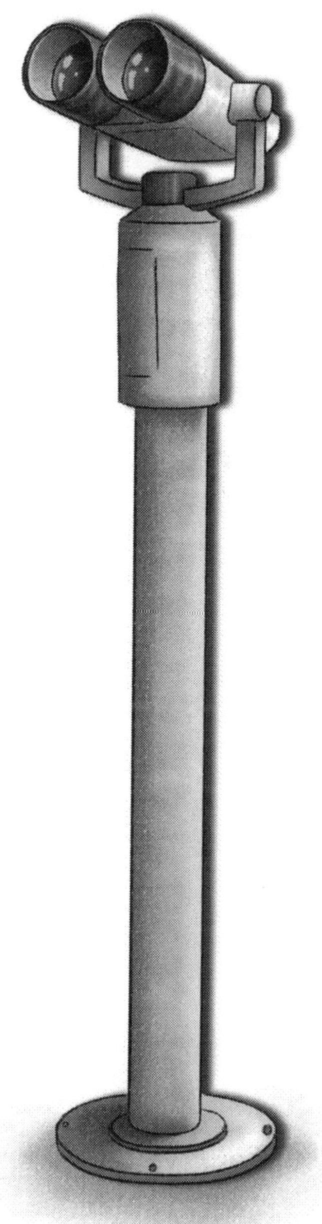

Ponder

What do you think these two women might discuss if they met?

What did today's reading tell you about the character or attitudes of Jesus?

What did today's reading tell you about how Jesus interacts with or responds to people?

What kind of a response (prayer, attitude, or action) does today's reading prompt within you?

Respond

Listening Jesus,

I thank you that you always hear my cries of desperation,

my silent prayers,

my whispered calls for help.

Out of the depths [of distress]
I have cried to You, O Lord.
Lord, hear my voice!
Let Your ears be attentive
To the voice of my supplications…
I wait [patiently] for the Lord,
my soul [expectantly] waits,
And in His word do I hope.
My soul waits for the Lord
More than the watchmen for the morning…
(Psalm 130:1-2, 5-6 AMP)

Day 10: Mark 6:1-31

...He did not hide his face from me
but heard when I cried to him. (Psalm 22:24)

He left there and returned to his hometown. His disciples came along. On the Sabbath, he gave a lecture in the meeting place. He stole the show, impressing everyone. "We had no idea he was this good!" they said. "How did he get so wise all of a sudden, get such ability?"

But in the next breath they were cutting him down: "He's just a carpenter—Mary's boy. We've known him since he was a kid. We know his brothers, James, Justus, Jude, and Simon, and his sisters. Who does he think he is?" They tripped over what little they knew about him and fell, sprawling. And they never got any further.

Jesus told them, "A prophet has little honor in his hometown, among his relatives, on the streets he played in as a child." Jesus wasn't able to do much of anything there—he laid hands on a few sick people and healed them, that's all. He couldn't get over their stubbornness. He left and made a circuit of the other villages, teaching.

Jesus called the Twelve to him, and sent them out in pairs. He gave them authority and power to deal with the evil opposition. He sent them off with these instructions: "Don't think you need a lot of extra equipment for this. You are the equipment. No special appeals for funds. Keep it simple. And no luxury inns. Get a modest place and be content there until you leave. If you're not welcomed, not listened to, quietly withdraw. Don't make a scene. Shrug your shoulders and be on your way."

Then they were on the road. They preached with joyful urgency that life can be radically different; right and left they sent the demons packing; they brought wellness to the sick, anointing their bodies, healing their spirits.

King Herod heard of all this, for by this time the name of Jesus was on everyone's lips. He said, "This has to be John the Baptizer come back from the dead—that's why he's able to work miracles!"

Others said, "No, it's Elijah." Others said, "He's a prophet, just like one of the old-time prophets."

But Herod wouldn't budge: "It's John, sure enough. I cut

off his head, and now he's back, alive."

[Herod was the one who had ordered the arrest of John, put him in chains, and sent him to prison at the nagging of Herodias, his brother Philip's wife. For John had provoked Herod by naming his relationship with Herodias "adultery." Herodias, smoldering with hate, wanted to kill him, but didn't dare because Herod was in awe of John. Convinced that he was a holy man, he gave him special treatment. Whenever he listened to him he was miserable with guilt—and yet he couldn't stay away. Something in John kept pulling him back.

But a portentous day arrived when Herod threw a birthday party, inviting all the brass and bluebloods in Galilee. Herodias's daughter entered the banquet hall and danced for the guests. She charmed Herod and the guests.

The king said to the girl, "Ask me anything. I'll give you anything you want." Carried away, he kept on, "I swear, I'll split my kingdom with you if you say so!"

She went back to her mother and said, "What should I ask for?"

"Ask for the head of John the Baptizer."

Excited, she ran back to the king and said, "I want the head of John the Baptizer served up on a platter. And I want it now!"

That sobered the king up fast. But unwilling to lose face with his guests, he caved in and let her have her wish. The king sent the executioner off to the prison with orders to bring back John's head. He went, cut off John's head, brought it back on a platter, and presented it to the girl, who gave it to her mother. When John's disciples heard about this, they came and got the body and gave it a decent burial.]

The apostles then rendezvoused with Jesus and reported on all that they had done and taught. Jesus said, "Come off by yourselves; let's take a break and get a little rest." For there was constant coming and going. They didn't even have time to eat. (MSG, brackets added)

Observe

Today's reading began with Jesus returning to Nazareth, where he was met with a mixed reception. The Message version sums up Jesus' reaction: "He couldn't get over their stubbornness."

Next, Jesus sent out his disciples in pairs to spread his message. Jesus' ministry had now grown to such an influential status that King Herod heard about it. Mark inserted some background information here, showing us Herod's fear that John the Baptist has returned to haunt him.

What stood out to me in this action-packed reading was the moment when the disciples returned to recount their ministry adventures to Jesus. I like the Message's phrase: "the apostles then rendezvoused with Jesus and reported on all that they had done and taught." Jesus listened to their accounts, and then urged them to join him for a time of well-deserved rest.

I don't know precisely what time of day the disciples had this meeting with Jesus, but I think it is a wonderful picture of evening prayer. Whether I follow a pattern of readings or simply take a few moments to review my day with Jesus, this practice can bring me peace. It doesn't always soothe all my worries away, but it helps me to drift off to sleep with the assurance of the Lord's presence with me.

Ponder

Imagine you are one of the disciples who has been watching and listening to Jesus. Suddenly he is sending you out with just one other disciple to spread his message. What emotions might you be feeling?

Respond

Keep watch, dear Lord, with those who work,
or watch, or weep this night,
and give your angels charge over those who sleep.
Tend the sick, Lord Christ; give rest to the weary,
bless the dying, soothe the suffering, pity the afflicted,
shield the joyous; and all for your love's sake. Amen.
–an evening prayer from the *Book of Common Prayer*

Yet the Lord will command His lovingkindness in the daytime,
And in the night His song will be with me,
A prayer to the God of my life. (Psalm 42:8 AMP)

Day 11: Mark 6:33-56

...He did not hide his face from me
but heard when I cried to him. (Psalm 22:24)

And they went away in the boat to a deserted place by themselves. Now many saw them going and recognized them, and they hurried there on foot from all the towns and arrived ahead of them. As he went ashore, he saw a great crowd, and he had compassion for them, because they were like sheep without a shepherd, and he began to teach them many things.

When it grew late, his disciples came to him and said, "This is a deserted place, and the hour is now very late; send them away so that they may go into the surrounding country and villages and buy something for themselves to eat."

But he answered them, "You give them something to eat."

They said to him, "Are we to go and buy two hundred denarii worth of bread and give it to them to eat?"

And he said to them, "How many loaves have you? Go and see."

When they had found out, they said, "Five, and two fish." Then he ordered them to get all the people to sit down in groups on the green grass. So they sat down in groups of hundreds and of fifties. Taking the five loaves and the two fish, he looked up to heaven and blessed and broke the loaves and gave them to his disciples to set before the people, and he divided the two fish among them all. And all ate and were filled, and they took up twelve baskets full of broken pieces and of the fish. Those who had eaten the loaves numbered five thousand men.

Immediately he made his disciples get into the boat and go on ahead to the other side, to Bethsaida, while he dismissed the crowd. After saying farewell to them, he went up on the mountain to pray.

When evening came, the boat was out on the sea, and he was alone on the land. When he saw that they were straining at the oars against an adverse wind, he came toward them early in the morning, walking on the sea. He intended to pass them by. But when they saw him walking on the sea, they thought it was a ghost and cried out, for they all saw him and were terrified. But immediately he spoke to them and said, "Take heart, it is I; do not be afraid." Then he got into the boat with them, and the wind ceased. And they were utterly astounded, for they did not understand about the loaves, but their hearts were hardened.

When they had crossed over, they came to land at Gennesaret and moored the boat. When they got out of the boat, people at once recognized him and rushed about that whole region and began to bring the sick on mats to wherever they heard he was. And wherever he went, into villages or cities or farms, they laid the sick in the marketplaces and begged him that they might touch even the fringe of his cloak, and all who touched it were healed.

Observe

Neither Jesus nor his disciples got the rest they were seeking at the end of yesterday's reading. Jesus' compassion kept him involved with the crowds of followers, caring for their spiritual needs as well as their physical hunger.

But the feeding of the crowd was not the only miracle that day. When a storm threatened the disciples, Jesus came to them, and as he got into their boat, the wind calmed.

Jesus' words to the storm-tossed disciples were simple and encouraging: "Take heart, it is I; do not be afraid." I have been using his words in my journal lately. I write out everything that is causing me stress and heartache, picturing all those things as waves, wind, and a vicious storm. And then I write down Jesus' words. I remember he is with me, and nothing is beyond his control. He is walking over all those troubles, all those storm-tossed waves, towards me.

Ponder

Why do you think the disciples so quickly forgot Jesus' power?

Respond

Jesus

You always listen to me with compassion,

and I am never an interruption to you.

You hear my cries of fear and my whispers of doubt,

and you respond with love and peace and your presence.

> *O Lord, You have heard the desire of the humble and oppressed; You will strengthen their heart, You will incline Your ear to hear. (Psalm 10:17 AMP)*

WEEK 3
Watch & Listen to the Reviving Jesus

Reading: Mark 7-9

Prayer

The law of the Lord is perfect,
reviving the soul. (Psalm 19:7)
The law of the Lord is perfect (flawless),
restoring and refreshing the soul;
The statutes of the Lord are reliable and trustworthy,
making wise the simple. (AMP)
The revelation of God is whole and pulls our lives together.
The signposts of God are clear and point out the right road.
The life-maps of God are right, showing the way to joy. (MSG)
The instructions of the Lord are perfect, reviving the soul.
The decrees of the Lord are trustworthy,
making wise the simple. (NLT)
The law of the Lord is perfect
and revives the soul. (BCP)

Define

Revive:

1. to activate, set in motion, or take up again; renew.
2. to restore to life or consciousness.[1]

Day 12: Mark 7:1-23

The law of the Lord is perfect, reviving the soul. (Psalm 19:7)

One day some Pharisees and teachers of religious law arrived from Jerusalem to see Jesus. They noticed that some of his disciples failed to follow the Jewish ritual of hand washing before eating. (The Jews, especially the Pharisees, do not eat until they have poured water over their cupped hands, as required by their ancient traditions. Similarly, they don't eat anything from the market until they immerse their hands in water. This is but one of many traditions they have clung to—such as their ceremonial washing of cups, pitchers, and kettles.)

So the Pharisees and teachers of religious law asked him, "Why don't your disciples follow our age-old tradition? They eat without first performing the hand-washing ceremony."

Jesus replied, "You hypocrites! Isaiah was right when he prophesied about you, for he wrote, 'These people honor me with their lips, but their hearts are far from me. Their worship is a farce, for they teach man-made ideas as commands from God.' For you ignore God's law and substitute your own tradition." Then he said, "You skillfully sidestep God's law in order to hold on to your own tradition. For instance, Moses gave you this law from God: 'Honor your father and mother,' and 'Anyone who speaks disrespectfully of father or mother must be put to death.' But you say it is all right for people to say to their parents, 'Sorry, I can't help you. For I have vowed to give to God what I would have given to you.' In this way, you let them disregard their needy parents. And so you cancel the word of God in order to hand down your own tradition. And this is only one example among many others."

Then Jesus called to the crowd to come and hear. "All of you listen," he said, "and try to understand. It's not what goes into your body that defiles you; you are defiled by what comes from your heart."

Then Jesus went into a house to get away from the crowd, and his disciples asked him what he meant by the parable he had just used. "Don't you understand either?" he asked. "Can't you see that the food you put into your body cannot defile you?

Food doesn't go into your heart, but only passes through the stomach and then goes into the sewer." (By saying this, he declared that every kind of food is acceptable in God's eyes.)

And then he added, "It is what comes from inside that defiles you. For from within, out of a person's heart, come evil thoughts, sexual immorality, theft, murder, adultery, greed, wickedness, deceit, lustful desires, envy, slander, pride, and foolishness. All these vile things come from within; they are what defile you." (NLT)

Define

hand-washing: Explained within the text, this ritual had little to do with sanitation, and was simply a religious tradition.

Observe

Jesus' quote from Isaiah really sums up this whole passage. He was interacting with people who were honoring God with their lips while their hearts were far from him. Their worship had become a farce, focused on their own traditions and feeding their own pride. They could not see past their rigid ways of worship to observe the Son of God himself calling them to repentance and revival.

Ponder

What might be a modern-day example of someone honoring God with their lips while their hearts are far from him?

Maybe you can think of a time when this phrase described your own worship. Isn't it encouraging to remember that we worship a God who revives us and who can breathe new life into us? We can always call out to him in prayer, asking him to revive our souls once again.

Respond

Revive my soul

Lord Jesus

that I may honor you with my whole heart,

my actions,

and my way of life.

> *This is my comfort in my affliction,*
> *That Your word has revived me and given me life.*
> *(Psalm 119:50 AMP)*

Day 13: Mark 7:24-8:10

The law of the Lord is perfect, reviving the soul. (Psalm 19:7)

From there he set out and went away to the region of Tyre. He entered a house and did not want anyone to know he was there. Yet he could not escape notice, but a woman whose little daughter had an unclean spirit immediately heard about him, and she came and bowed down at his feet. Now the woman was a gentile, of Syrophoenician origin. She begged him to cast the demon out of her daughter. He said to her, "Let the children be fed first, for it is not fair to take the children's food and throw it to the dogs."

But she answered him, "Sir, even the dogs under the table eat the children's crumbs."

Then he said to her, "For saying that, you may go—the demon has left your daughter." And when she went home, she found the child lying on the bed and the demon gone.

Then he returned from the region of Tyre and went by way of Sidon toward the Sea of Galilee, in the region of the Decapolis. They brought to him a deaf man who had an impediment in his speech, and they begged him to lay his hand on him. He took him aside in private, away from the crowd, and put his fingers into his ears, and he spat and touched his tongue. Then looking up to heaven, he sighed and said to him, "Ephphatha," that is, "Be opened." And his ears were opened, his tongue was released, and he spoke plainly.

Then Jesus ordered them to tell no one, but the more he ordered them, the more zealously they proclaimed it. They were astounded beyond measure, saying, "He has done everything well; he even makes the deaf to hear and the mute to speak."

In those days when there was again a great crowd without anything to eat, he called his disciples and said to them, "I have compassion for the crowd because they have been with me now for three days and have nothing to eat. If I send them away hungry to their homes, they will faint on the way—and some of them have come from a great distance."

His disciples replied, "How can one feed these people with bread here in the desert?"

He asked them, "How many loaves do you have?" They

said, "Seven."

Then he ordered the crowd to sit down on the ground, and he took the seven loaves, and after giving thanks he broke them and gave them to his disciples to distribute, and they distributed them to the crowd. They had also a few small fish, and after blessing them he ordered that these, too, should be distributed. They ate and were filled, and they took up the broken pieces left over, seven baskets full. Now there were about four thousand people. And he sent them away. And immediately he got into the boat with his disciples and went to the district of Dalmanutha.

Define

Syrophoenician: The woman was from a region in Phoenicia that was under the control of Syria.

Observe

The conversation between Jesus and the Syrophoenician woman is puzzling. Some scholars suggest that Jesus, like many of us, occasionally used a little sarcasm. If you read this scene with a sarcastic tone, you hear the woman and Jesus having a conversation that reflected the political and religious views of their time—views they themselves did not hold. I imagine them gesturing with whatever the first-century equivalent of air quotes might be.

Regardless of your viewpoint on this passage, it is obvious that Jesus responded to the determined attitude of this woman who loved her child dearly.

This passage held one miracle after another: healings and a miraculously multiplying meal. I love the phrase, "He has done everything well." We never have to worry that we will bring a need to Jesus that he cannot handle.

Ponder

How do you see Jesus reviving people in this passage?

Respond

Reviving Jesus,

I see you offering opportunities for new ways of life

to people in all walks of life.

You do everything well,

and I can trust you to bring new life to me.

> *So if anyone is in Christ, there is a new creation:*
> *everything old has passed away;*
> *look, new things have come into being! (2 Corinthians 5:17)*

Day 14: Mark 8:11-38

The law of the Lord is perfect, reviving the soul. (Psalm 19:7)

The Pharisees came out and began to argue [contentiously and debate] with Him, demanding from Him a sign from heaven, to test Him [because of their unbelief]. He groaned and sighed deeply in His spirit and said, "Why does this generation demand a sign? I assure you and most solemnly say to you, no sign will be given to this generation!" Leaving them, He again boarded the boat and left for the other side.

Now the disciples had forgotten to bring bread, and they had only one loaf with them in the boat. Jesus repeatedly ordered them, saying, "Watch out! Beware of the leaven of the Pharisees and the leaven of Herod."

They began discussing this with one another, saying, "It is because we have no bread [that He said this]."

Jesus, aware of this [discussion], said to them, "Why are you discussing [the fact] that you have no bread? Do you still not see or understand? Are your hearts hardened? Though you have eyes, do you not see? And though you have ears, do you not hear and listen [to what I have said]? And do you not remember, when I broke the five loaves for the five thousand, how many baskets full of broken pieces you picked up?"

They answered, "Twelve."

"And [when I broke] the seven [loaves] for the four thousand, how many large baskets full of broken pieces did you pick up?"

And they answered, "Seven."

And He was saying to them, "Do you still not understand?"

Then they came to Bethsaida; and some people brought a blind man to Jesus and begged Him to touch him. Taking the blind man by the hand, He led him out of the village; and after spitting on his eyes and laying His hands on him, He asked him, "Do you see anything?"

And he looked up and said, "I see people, but [they look] like trees, walking around."

Then again Jesus laid His hands on his eyes; and the man stared intently and [his sight] was [completely] restored, and he began to see everything clearly. And He sent him to his home, saying, "Do not even enter the village."

Then Jesus and His disciples went out to the villages of [Caesarea Philippi; and on the way He asked His disciples, "Who do people say that I am?"

They answered Him, "John the Baptist; and others say Elijah; but others, one of the prophets."

And He asked them, "But who do you say that I am?"

Peter replied to Him, "You [in contrast to the others] are the Christ (the Messiah, the Anointed)."

Then Jesus strictly warned them not to tell anyone about Him. And He began to teach them that the Son of Man must [of necessity] suffer many things and be rejected [as the Messiah] by the elders and the chief priests and the scribes, and must be put to death, and after three days rise [from death to life]. He was stating the matter plainly [not holding anything back].

Then Peter took Him aside and began to reprimand Him. But turning around [with His back to Peter] and seeing His disciples, He rebuked Peter, saying, "Get behind Me, Satan; for your mind is not set on God's will or His values and purposes, but on what pleases man."

Jesus called the crowd together with His disciples, and said to them, "If anyone wishes to follow Me [as My disciple], he must deny himself [set aside selfish interests], and take up his cross [expressing a willingness to endure whatever may come] and follow Me [believing in Me, conforming to My example in living and, if need be, suffering or perhaps dying because of faith in Me]. For whoever wishes to save his life [in this world] will [eventually] lose it [through death], but whoever loses his life [in this world] for My sake and the gospel's will save it [from the consequences of sin and separation from God]. For what does it benefit a man to gain the whole world [with all its pleasures], and forfeit his soul? For what will a man give in exchange for his soul and eternal life [in God's kingdom]? For whoever is ashamed [here and now] of Me and My words in this adulterous and sinful generation, the Son of Man will also be ashamed of him when He comes in the glory of His Father with the holy angels." (AMP) leaven: "A substance such as yeast that consists mostly of fungi. This analogy relates the impurity of a leavening agent to the impurity of the man-made tradition and hypocrisy of the Pharisees that was preventing the nation of Israel from accepting the Messiah."[2]

Observe

I was encouraged when I observed the Apostle Peter in today's reading. He expressed the great spiritual truth about Jesus' identity, but in the next breath he reprimanded Jesus, presuming to know the future better than Jesus did.

I am grateful that the gospels show us the humanity and the failures of the Apostles. It is reassuring to see that God uses imperfect people – because that is exactly who we all are! We all need his reviving spirit to empower us to follow him.

Ponder

> *Jesus called the crowd together with His disciples, and said to them, "If anyone wishes to follow Me [as My disciple], he must deny himself [set aside selfish interests], and take up his cross [expressing a willingness to endure whatever may come] and follow Me…" (Mark 8:34 AMP)*

How would you put Jesus' instructions in this verse into your own words?

Respond

Reviving Jesus,

When I don't understand your plan

and when spiritual truth seems cloudy

I take comfort

in simply being aware of your presence.

> *Your promise revives me;*
> *it comforts me in all my troubles.*
> *(Psalm 119:50 NLT)*

Day 15: Mark 9:1-32

The law of the Lord is perfect, reviving the soul. (Psalm 19:7)

And he said to them, "Truly I tell you, there are some standing here who will not taste death until they see that the kingdom of God has come with power."

Six days later, Jesus took with him Peter and James and John and led them up a high mountain apart, by themselves. And he was transfigured before them, and his clothes became dazzling bright, such as no one on earth could brighten them. And there appeared to them Elijah with Moses, who were talking with Jesus.

Then Peter said to Jesus, "Rabbi, it is good for us to be here; let us set up three tents: one for you, one for Moses, and one for Elijah." He did not know what to say, for they were terrified.

Then a cloud overshadowed them, and from the cloud there came a voice, "This is my Son, the Beloved; listen to him!" Suddenly when they looked around, they saw no one with them any more, but only Jesus.

As they were coming down the mountain, he ordered them to tell no one about what they had seen, until after the Son of Man had risen from the dead. So they kept the matter to themselves, questioning what this rising from the dead could mean. Then they asked him, "Why do the scribes say that Elijah must come first?"

He said to them, "Elijah is indeed coming first to restore all things. How then is it written about the Son of Man, that he is to go through many sufferings and be treated with contempt? But I tell you that Elijah has come, and they did to him whatever they pleased, as it is written about him."

When they came to the disciples, they saw a great crowd around them and some

scribes arguing with them. When the whole crowd saw him, they were immediately overcome with awe, and they ran forward to greet him. He asked them, "What are you arguing about with them?"

Someone from the crowd answered him, "Teacher, I brought you my son; he has a spirit that makes him unable to speak, and whenever it seizes him, it dashes him down, and he foams and grinds his teeth and becomes rigid, and I asked your disciples to cast it out, but they could not do so."

He answered them, "You faithless generation, how much longer must I be with you? How much longer must I put up with you? Bring him to me."

And they brought the boy to him. When the spirit saw him, immediately it convulsed the boy, and he fell on the ground and rolled about, foaming at the mouth. Jesus asked the father, "How long has this been happening to him?"

And he said, "From childhood. It has often cast him into the fire and into the water, to destroy him; but if you are able to do anything, help us! Have compassion on us!"

Jesus said to him, "If you are able! All things can be done for the one who believes."

Immediately the father of the child cried out, "I believe; help my unbelief!"

When Jesus saw that a crowd came running together, he rebuked the unclean spirit, saying to it, "You spirit that keeps this boy from speaking and hearing, I command you, come out of him, and never enter him again!"

After crying out and convulsing him terribly, it came out, and the boy was like a corpse, so that most of them said, "He is dead." But Jesus took him by the hand and lifted him up, and he was able to stand.

When he had entered the house, his disciples asked him privately, "Why could we not cast it out?"

He said to them, "This kind can come out only through prayer."

Observe

This passage has a little of everything, from the glorious Transfiguration to the simple faith of a man who believed yet

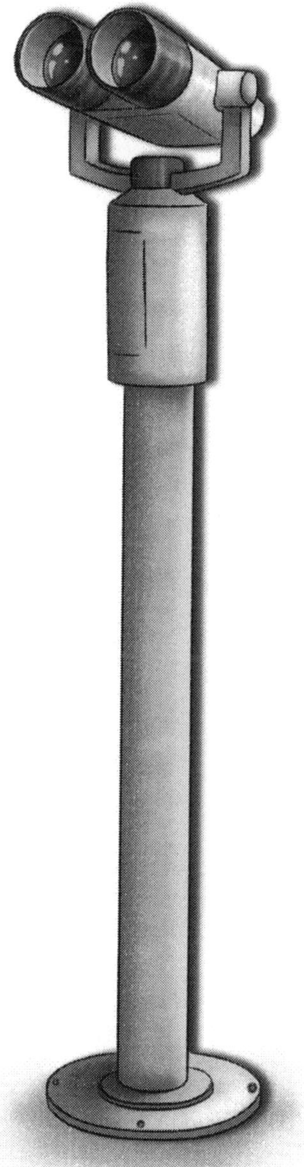

asked for assistance with his unbelief.

Peter's comment about building tents makes sense when we remember Jewish history, and the Tabernacle tent that held God's glory. But Jesus didn't come to earth to live in a remote tent, out of our reach. He walked back down the mountain with his disciples, back to the routines and challenges of life.

They didn't have time to rest or bask in the memory of what they had just seen. They were met by a desperate father and son who were seeking deliverance from a situation beyond their control. It is so beautiful to see Jesus respond to the father's heartfelt cry. This simple prayer can be helpful in our own prayers as we speak to the Lord with simple honesty.

... I believe; help my unbelief! (Mark 9:24)

Ponder

In what other situation did God the Father speak of Jesus as his beloved son? (See page 5.)

Why do you think God the Father chose to speak audibly at these two events?

Consider the three men who saw Jesus' glory in this passage. Peter would go on to be one of the leaders in the early church. James would be one of the earliest martyrs. John would outlive all of the other disciples, going on to write letters to churches as well as his great Revelation. How do you think this glimpse of Jesus' glory at the Transfiguration encouraged these men as their lives unfolded?

Respond

Revival can be scary, Lord
as you urge me to make changes
and begin new habits
while you show me
occasional glimpses of glory.
When I don't understand
and when I don't know what to say,
I can echo the desperate father
and whisper
"I do believe. Help my unbelief."

> *…You who seek God*
> *[requiring Him as your greatest need],*
> *let your heart revive and live.*
> *For the Lord hears the needy…* *(Psalm 69:32-33 AMP)*

Day 16: Mark 9:33-50

The law of the Lord is perfect, reviving the soul. (Psalm 19:7)

Then they came to Capernaum, and when he was in the house he asked them, "What were you arguing about on the way?" But they were silent, for on the way they had argued with one another who was the greatest.

He sat down, called the twelve, and said to them, "Whoever wants to be first must be last of all and servant of all." Then he took a little child and put it among them, and taking it in his arms he said to them, "Whoever welcomes one such child in my name welcomes me, and whoever welcomes me welcomes not me but the one who sent me."

John said to him, "Teacher, we saw someone casting out demons in your name, and we tried to stop him because he was not following us."

But Jesus said, "Do not stop him, for no one who does a deed of power in my name will be able soon afterward to speak evil of me. Whoever is not against us is for us. For truly I tell you, whoever gives you a cup of water to drink because you bear the name of Christ will by no means lose the reward.

"If any of you cause one of these little ones who believe in me to sin, it would be better for you if a great millstone were hung around your neck and you were thrown into the sea. If your hand causes you to sin, cut it off; it is better for you to enter life maimed than to have two hands and to go to hell, to the unquenchable fire. And if your foot causes you to sin, cut it off; it is better for you to enter life lame than to have two feet and to be thrown into hell. And if your eye causes you to sin, tear it out; it is better for you to enter the kingdom of God with one eye than to have two eyes and to be thrown into hell, where their worm never dies and the fire is never quenched.

"For everyone will be salted with fire. Salt is good, but if salt has lost its saltiness, how can you season it? Have salt in yourselves, and be at peace with one another."

Observe

The disciples were expecting great things like power and miracles, but Jesus redirected them to an inner revival and a new system of values. In this new life, humility is foundational, a sense of our own powerlessness and immaturity is needed, and we must make great sacrifices to avoid evil.

The words about removing body parts are hyperbole – graphic and exaggerated statements to catch our attention.

Ponder

How would you describe Jesus in this passage? What is his attitude? How does he interact with his disciples?

Respond

Reviving Jesus,
Help me to remember that my faith journey
is so much bigger
than simply finding my own personal fulfillment.
You are active in this world
–and so are the forces of evil–
and you call me to cooperate with you
to spread the news of your kingdom
and your love
and your revival.

Revive me according to Your lovingkindness,
so that I may keep the testimony of Your mouth.
(Psalm 119:88 NKJV)

WEEK 4
Watch & Listen to the Steadfastly Loving Jesus

Reading: Mark 10-12

Prayer

Let them thank the Lord for his steadfast love,
for his wonderful works to humankind. (Psalm 107:21)
Let them give thanks to the Lord for His lovingkindness,
And for His wonderful acts to the children of men! (AMP)
So thank God for his marvelous love,
for his miracle mercy to the children he loves. (MSG)
Let them praise the Lord for his great love
and for the wonderful things he has done for them. (NLT)
Let them give thanks to the Lord for his mercy
and the wonders he does for his children. (BCP)

Define

steadfast love: in the Hebrew language of Psalm 107:21, "streadfast love" is *hesed*. This word means goodness, kindness, and faithfulness.[1]

Day 17: Mark 10:1-31

Let them thank the Lord for his steadfast love,
for his wonderful works to humankind. (Psalm 107:21)

He left that place and went to the region of Judea and beyond the Jordan. And crowds again gathered around him, and, as was his custom, he again taught them. Some, testing him, asked, "Is it lawful for a man to divorce his wife?"

He answered them, "What did Moses command you?"

They said, "Moses allowed a man to write a certificate of dismissal and to divorce her."

But Jesus said to them, "Because of your hardness of heart he wrote this commandment for you. But from the beginning of creation, 'God made them male and female.' 'For this reason a man shall leave his father and mother and be joined to his wife, and the two shall become one flesh.' So they are no longer two but one flesh. Therefore what God has joined together, let no one separate."

Then in the house the disciples asked him again about this matter. He said to them, "Whoever divorces his wife and marries another commits adultery against her, and if she divorces her husband and marries another, she commits adultery."

People were bringing children to him in order that he might touch them, and the disciples spoke sternly to them. But when Jesus saw this, he was indignant and said to them, "Let the children come to me; do not stop them, for it is to such as these that the kingdom of God belongs. Truly I tell you, whoever does not receive the kingdom of God as a little child will never enter it." And he took them up in his arms, laid his hands on them, and blessed them.

As he was setting out on a journey, a man ran up and knelt before him and asked him, "Good Teacher, what must I do to inherit eternal life?"

Jesus said to him, "Why do you call me good? No one is good but God alone. You know the commandments: 'You shall not murder. You shall not commit adultery. You shall not steal. You shall not bear false witness. You shall not defraud. Honor your father and mother.' "

He said to him, "Teacher, I have kept all these since my youth."

Jesus, looking at him, loved him and said, "You lack one thing; go, sell what you own, and give the money to the poor, and you will have treasure in heaven; then come, follow me."

When he heard this, he was shocked and went away grieving, for he had many possessions.

Then Jesus looked around and said to his disciples, "How hard it will be for those who have wealth to enter the kingdom of God!" And the disciples were perplexed at these words. But Jesus said to them again, "Children, how hard it is to enter the kingdom of God! It is easier for a camel to go through the eye of a needle than for someone who is rich to enter the kingdom of God."

They were greatly astounded and said to one another, "Then who can be saved?"

Jesus looked at them and said, "For mortals it is impossible, but not for God; for God all things are possible."

Peter began to say to him, "Look, we have left everything and followed you."

Jesus said, "Truly I tell you, there is no one who has left house or brothers or sisters or mother or father or children or fields for my sake and for the sake of the good news who will not receive a hundredfold now in this age—houses, brothers and sisters, mothers and children, and fields, with persecutions—and in the age to come eternal life. But many who are first will be last, and the last will be first."

Define

divorce: In our modern culture, divorce can provide safety and an escape for individuals in difficult and harmful situations. In the culture of Jesus' day, divorce was very different. While men could divorce their wives for the smallest of reasons, women could not even initiate a divorce. Because there were so few opportunities for single women to support themselves, divorced women were often doomed to lives of extreme poverty or forced into prostitution. In this passage, Jesus was talking to men who were intensely proud of the way they followed every detail of their religious laws. Jesus urged them to look beyond the issue of whether divorce was legal to consider its impact on those affected by it.

Observe

I think the last sentence of this selection interprets the whole thing. Jesus wants us to have a simple trust in Him and to put Him first in our lives. He encourages us to cherish those whom society may overlook and not to be too attached to our belongings. He calls us to rely on God for our needs and our sense of value, always remembering and echoing his steadfast love.

Isn't it interesting that we are not told the outcome of Jesus' conversation with the young man? Many people presume the man did not follow Jesus' advice, but I like to think that he eventually did. Perhaps he "went away grieving" because he was deeply conscious of what it was going to cost him to follow Jesus.

Ponder

Choose one of the following familiar statements of Jesus from today's passage:

- "Receive the kingdom of God as a little child."
- "For God all things are possible."
- "Many who are first will be last, and the last will be first."

Look back at the reading to see the context (what was the situation, who was Jesus talking to, and what was he talking about).

Now consider how you would put this statement into your own words.

Respond

Jesus,

in your steadfast love you care for everyone:

those in positions of wealth and influence who sought to trick you,

the seekers who approached you with genuine inquiries,

the women and children overlooked by society,

and your devoted disciples who, in their imperfect human nature,

walked alongside you.

> *How precious is your steadfast love, O God!*
> *All people may take refuge in the shadow of your wings.*
> *(Psalm 36:7)*

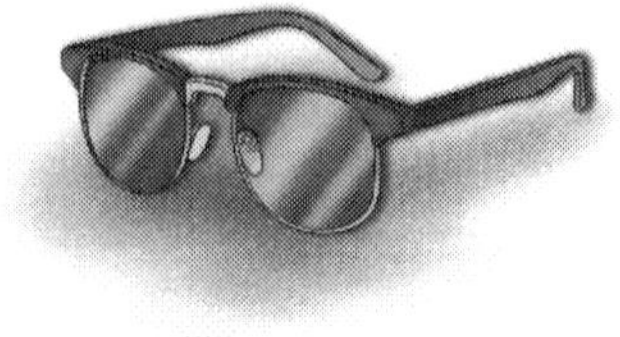

Day 18: Mark 10:32-52

Let them thank the Lord for his steadfast love, for his wonderful works to humankind. (Psalm 107:21)

Now they were on the road going up to Jerusalem, and Jesus was walking on ahead of them; and they were perplexed [at what Jesus had said], and those who were following were alarmed and afraid. And again He took the twelve [disciples] aside and began telling them what was going to happen to Him, saying, "Listen very carefully: we are going up to Jerusalem, and the Son of Man will be betrayed and handed over to the chief priests and the scribes; and they will condemn Him to death and hand Him over to the Gentiles (Romans). They will mock and ridicule Him and spit on Him, and whip (scourge) Him and kill Him, and three days later He will rise [from the dead]."

James and John, the two sons of Zebedee, came to Him, saying, "Teacher, we want You to do for us whatever we ask of You."

And He replied to them, "What do you want Me to do for you?"

They said to Him, "Grant that we may sit [with You], one on Your right and one on Your left, in Your glory [Your majesty and splendor in Your kingdom]."

But Jesus said to them, "You do not know what you are asking. Are you able to drink the cup that I drink, or to be baptized with the baptism [of suffering and death] with which I am baptized?"

And they replied to Him, "We are able."

Jesus told them, "The cup that I drink you will drink, and you will be baptized with the baptism with which I am baptized. But to sit on My right or left, this is not Mine to give; but it is for those for whom it has been prepared [by My Father]."

Hearing this, the [other] ten became indignant with James and John. Calling them to

Himself, Jesus said to them, "You know that those who are recognized as rulers of the Gentiles lord it over them; and their powerful men exercise authority over them [tyrannizing them]. But this is not how it is among you; instead, whoever wishes to become great among you must be your servant, and whoever wishes to be first and most important among you must be slave of all. For even the Son of Man did not come to be served, but to serve, and to give His life as a ransom for many."

Then they came to Jericho. And as He was leaving Jericho with His disciples and a large crowd, a blind beggar, Bartimaeus, the son of Timaeus, was sitting beside the road [as was his custom]. When Bartimaeus heard that it was Jesus of Nazareth, he began to shout and say, "Jesus, Son of David (Messiah), have mercy on me!" Many sternly rebuked him, telling him to keep still and be quiet; but he kept on shouting out all the more, "Son of David (Messiah), have mercy on me!"

Jesus stopped and said, "Call him."

So they called the blind man, telling him, "Take courage, get up! He is calling for you." Throwing his cloak aside, he jumped up and came to Jesus.

And Jesus said, "What do you want Me to do for you?"

The blind man said to Him, "Rabboni (my Master), let me regain my sight."

Jesus said to him, "Go; your faith [and confident trust in My power] has made you well." Immediately he regained his sight and began following Jesus on the road. (AMP)

Define

they were on the road going up to Jerusalem: Jesus was now making his final pilgrimage to Jerusalem for the Passover.

to give his life as a ransom for many: The Amplified Bible has a footnote that explains this to mean, "to die so that believers may be freed from the power of sin and death."[2]

Observe

James and John had preconceived ideas about how the Messiah would act and what his future would hold. No matter how often Jesus foretold his sacrifice, they continued to concentrate on a powerful future for themselves.

> *Whoever wishes to become great among you must be your servant, and whoever wishes to be first and most important among you must be slave of all. For even the Son of Man did not come to be served, but to serve, and to give His life as a ransom for many. (Mark 10:43-45 AMP)*

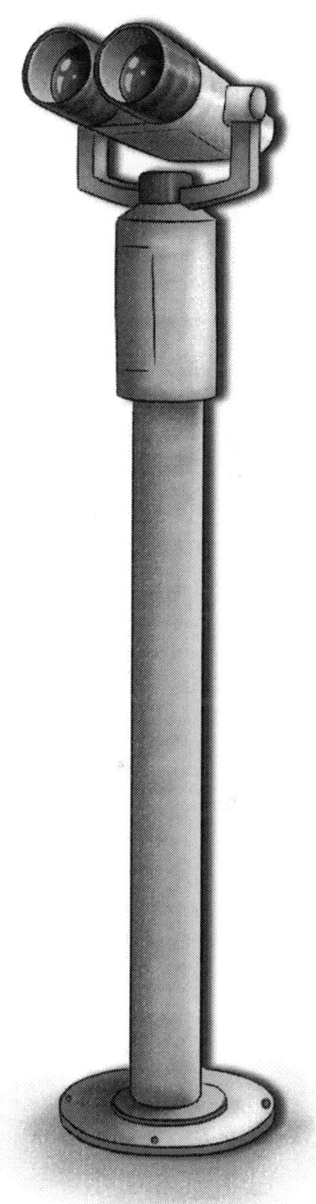

These verses sum up the portrait of Jesus that emerges from the book of Mark: a Messiah who serves, who acts, who reaches out with love and compassion.

Ponder

What did Bartimaeus do as soon as he was healed?

How would you describe Jesus in this passage? What are his character qualities and attributes?

How does Jesus interact with people in this passage?

How would you summarize Jesus' message or instructions in this passage?

Respond

"Take courage, get up! He is calling for you!"

I hear you calling, Lord.

You speak of embracing

humility and servitude,

of drinking cups

filled with adversity and hardship.

Yet, you assure me of your presence

beside me

along the rugged journey of life.

You are my vision, my courage,

and my friend.

But I will sing of your might;
I will sing aloud of your steadfast love in the morning.
For you have been a fortress for me
and a refuge in the day of my distress. (Psalm 59:16)

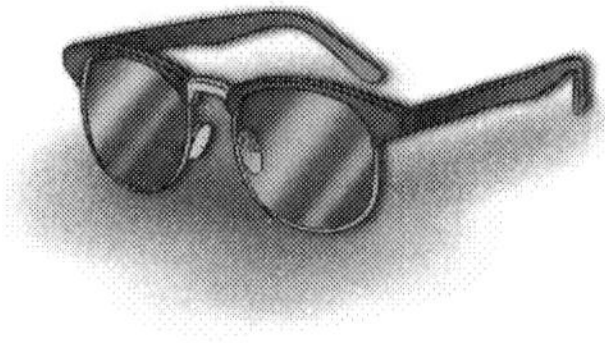

Day 19: Mark 11

Let them thank the Lord for his steadfast love, for his wonderful works to humankind. (Psalm 107:21)

As Jesus and his disciples approached Jerusalem, they came to the towns of Bethphage and Bethany on the Mount of Olives. Jesus sent two of them on ahead. "Go into that village over there," he told them. "As soon as you enter it, you will see a young donkey tied there that no one has ever ridden. Untie it and bring it here. If anyone asks, 'What are you doing?' just say, 'The Lord needs it and will return it soon.'"

The two disciples left and found the colt standing in the street, tied outside the front door. As they were untying it, some bystanders demanded, "What are you doing, untying that colt?" They said what Jesus had told them to say, and they were permitted to take it. Then they brought the colt to Jesus and threw their garments over it, and he sat on it. Many in the crowd spread their garments on the road ahead of him, and others spread leafy branches they had cut in the fields.

Jesus was in the center of the procession, and the people all around him were shouting, "Praise God! Blessings on the one who comes in the name of the Lord! Blessings on the coming Kingdom of our ancestor David! Praise God in highest heaven!"

So Jesus came to Jerusalem and went into the Temple. After looking around carefully at everything, he left because it was late in the afternoon. Then he returned to Bethany with the twelve disciples.

The next morning as they were leaving Bethany, Jesus was hungry. He noticed a fig tree in full leaf a little way off, so he went over to see if he could find any figs. But there were only leaves because it was too early in the season for fruit. Then Jesus said to the tree, "May no one ever eat your fruit again!" And the disciples heard him say it.

When they arrived back in Jerusalem, Jesus entered the Temple and began to drive out the people buying and selling animals for sacrifices. He knocked over the tables of the money changers and the chairs of those selling doves, and he stopped everyone from using the Temple as a marketplace. He said to them, "The Scriptures declare, 'My Temple will be called a house of prayer for all nations,' but you have turned it into a den of thieves."

When the leading priests and teachers of religious law heard what Jesus had done, they began planning how to kill him. But they were afraid of him because the people were so amazed at his teaching.

That evening Jesus and the disciples left the city. The next morning as they passed by the fig tree he had cursed, the disciples noticed it had withered from the roots up. Peter remembered what Jesus had said to the tree on the previous day and exclaimed, "Look, Rabbi! The fig tree you cursed has withered and died!"

Then Jesus said to the disciples, "Have faith in God. I tell you the truth, you can say to this mountain, 'May you be lifted up and thrown into the sea,' and it will happen. But you must really believe it will happen and have no doubt in your heart. I tell you, you can pray for anything, and if you believe that you've received it, it will be yours. But when you are praying, first forgive anyone you are holding a grudge against, so that your Father in heaven will forgive your sins, too."

Again they entered Jerusalem. As Jesus was walking through the Temple area, the leading priests, the teachers of religious law, and the elders came up to him. They demanded, "By what authority are you doing all these things? Who gave you the right to do them?"

"I'll tell you by what authority I do these things if you answer one question," Jesus replied. "Did John's authority to baptize come from heaven, or was it merely human? Answer me!"

They talked it over among themselves. "If we say it was from heaven, he will ask why we didn't believe John. But do we dare say it was merely human?" For they were afraid of what the people would do, because everyone believed that John was a prophet. So they finally replied, "We don't know."

And Jesus responded, "Then I won't tell you by what authority I do these things." (NLT)

Define

hosanna: When we read about Jesus' entry into Jerusalem, we often read that the crowd shouted "Hosanna!" The New

Living Translation uses the English translation of this Hebrew word: "Praise God in the highest heaven!"

a house of prayer for all nations: The temple had a single area for non-Jewish visitors to pray. If money-changers and animal sellers occupied this space, it would create a disruptive and environment for those seeking a place for worship and prayer.

Observe

As the promised Messiah, the King, approached his capital city, the streets were full of celebration and praise. But the scene and the mood quickly shifted. A holy place of prayer had become a market place, and the leaders of religion were looking for a reason to kill the king of life. Jesus looked at the scene carefully, and returned the next day to emphatically interrupt the market.

N. T. Wright describes Jesus' actions with the fig tree as an "acted parable."[3] Jesus came to a nation that claimed to anticipate the Messiah. While he was embraced by crowds of people, the power-hungry leaders sought only to destroy him. They were like an unfruitful tree – not fulfilling their purpose.

Ponder

Picture yourself as the owner of the donkey. How would you respond when the disciples (perhaps strangers to you) took the donkey away with a simple statement that the Lord needs it?

Respond

Loving Jesus,

as I approach the readings of your suffering and sacrifice,

soften my heart with your steadfast love,

that I may respond to you in gratefulness

and echo your attitude of forgiveness.

> *For you, O Lord, are good and forgiving,*
> *abounding in steadfast love to all who call on you.*
> *(Psalm 86:5)*

Day 20: Mark 12:1-27

Let them thank the Lord for his steadfast love, for his wonderful works to humankind. (Psalm 107:21)

Then he began to speak to them in parables. "A man planted a vineyard, put a fence around it, dug a pit for the winepress, and built a watchtower; then he leased it to tenants and went away. When the season came, he sent a slave to the tenants to collect from them his share of the produce of the vineyard. But they seized him and beat him and sent him away empty-handed. And again he sent another slave to them; this one they beat over the head and insulted. Then he sent another, and that one they killed. And so it was with many others; some they beat, and others they killed. He had still one other, a beloved son. Finally he sent him to them, saying, 'They will respect my son.' But those tenants said to one another, 'This is the heir; come, let us kill him, and the inheritance will be ours.' So they seized him, killed him, and threw him out of the vineyard. What then will the owner of the vineyard do? He will come and destroy the tenants and give the vineyard to others. Have you not read this scripture: 'The stone that the builders rejected has become the cornerstone; this was the Lord's doing, and it is amazing in our eyes'?"

When they realized that he had told this parable against them, they wanted to arrest him, but they feared the crowd. So they left him and went away.

Then they sent to him some Pharisees and some Herodians to trap him in what he said. And they came and said to him, "Teacher, we know that you are sincere and show deference to no one, for you do not regard people with partiality but teach the way of God in accordance with truth. Is it lawful to pay taxes to Caesar or not? Should we pay them, or should we not?"

But knowing their hypocrisy, he said to them, "Why are you putting me to the test? Bring me a denarius and let me see it." And they brought one. Then he said to them, "Whose head is this and whose title?"

They answered, "Caesar's."

Jesus said to them, "Give to Caesar the things that are Caesar's and to God the things that are God's." And they were utterly amazed at him.

Some Sadducees, who say there is no resurrection, came to him and asked him a question, saying, "Teacher, Moses wrote for us that if a man's brother dies, leaving a wife but no child, the man shall marry the widow and raise up children for his brother. There were seven brothers; the first married and, when he died, left no children, and the second married the widow and died, leaving no children, and the third likewise; none of the seven left children. Last of all the woman herself died. In the resurrection, when they rise, whose wife will she be? For all seven had married her."

Jesus said to them, "Is not this the reason you are wrong, that you know neither the scriptures nor the power of God? For when people rise from the dead, they neither marry nor are given in marriage but are like angels in heaven. And as for the dead being raised, have you not read in the book of Moses, in the story about the bush, how God said to him, 'I am the God of Abraham, the God of Isaac, and the God of Jacob'? He is God not of the dead but of the living; you are quite wrong."

Define

Sadducees: this group of religious leaders did not believe in life after death. They were rarely in agreement with the Pharisees. So, when we observe these factions collaborating to eliminate Jesus, it gives us a sense of how determined they were to get rid of him.

Observe

I am fascinated by Jesus' description of the "God of Abraham, the God of Isaac, and the God of Jacob." If you are familiar with Old Testament history, you know that Abraham, Isaac, and Jacob were far from perfect examples of morality. They struggled to have faith, they told lies, and they manipulated people. Still, God identified Himself as their God.

When Jesus came to the world, He spoke to gatherings that included a mix of people—some eager to listen and others trying to deceive Him. They were all ordinary, imperfect human beings, and Jesus loved them all.

God so loved the world that he gave his only Son, so that everyone who believes in him may not perish but may have eternal life. (John 3:16)

Ponder

I really like the way the Message version puts Jesus' words, recalling God's words to Moses at the burning bush in Exodus:

God at the bush said to Moses, 'I am—not was—the God of Abraham, the God of Isaac, and the God of Jacob'? The living God is God of the living, not the dead. (Mark 12:27 MSG)

Think about the Lord describing himself as "I am." Not "I was." Not "someday I will be." How does that impact you today?

Respond

Loving Jesus,
When I read of you as the "I am"
I see that you are the God of today,
even if my day seems out of control
and I cannot see where you are guiding me,
I can trust you.
Lord I believe.
Help my unbelief.

O my strength, I will sing praises to you,
for you, O God, are my fortress,
the God who shows me steadfast love. (Psalm 59:17)

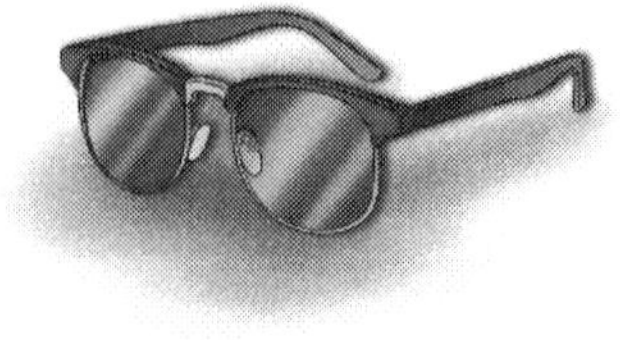

Day 21: Mark 12:28-44

Let them thank the Lord for his steadfast love, for his wonderful works to humankind. (Psalm 107:21)

One of the scribes came near and heard them disputing with one another, and seeing that he answered them well he asked him, "Which commandment is the first of all?"

Jesus answered, "The first is, 'Hear, O Israel: the Lord our God, the Lord is one; you shall love the Lord your God with all your heart and with all your soul and with all your mind and with all your strength.' The second is this, 'You shall love your neighbor as yourself.' There is no other commandment greater than these."

Then the scribe said to him, "You are right, Teacher; you have truly said that 'he is one, and besides him there is no other'; and 'to love him with all the heart and with all the understanding and with all the strength' and 'to love one's neighbor as oneself'—this is much more important than all whole burnt offerings and sacrifices."

When Jesus saw that he answered wisely, he said to him, "You are not far from the kingdom of God." After that no one dared to ask him any question.

While Jesus was teaching in the temple, he said, "How can the scribes say that the Messiah is the son of David? David himself, by the Holy Spirit, declared, 'The Lord said to my Lord, "Sit at my right hand, until I put your enemies under your feet." ' David himself calls him Lord, so how can he be his son?" And the large crowd was listening to him with delight.

As he taught, he said, "Beware of the scribes, who like to walk around in long robes and to be greeted with respect in the marketplaces and to have the best seats in the synagogues and places of honor at banquets! They devour widows' houses and for the sake of appearance say long prayers. They will receive the greater condemnation."

He sat down opposite the treasury and watched the crowd putting money into the treasury. Many rich people put in large sums. A poor widow came and put in two small copper coins, which are worth a penny. Then he called his disciples and said to them, "Truly I tell you, this poor widow has put in more than all those who are contributing to the treasury. For all of them have contributed out of their abundance, but she out of her poverty has put in everything she had, all she had to live on."

Observe

Jesus warned his listeners about religious leaders who were focused on their own gains and their own power. Then he pointed out someone worthy of respect – a widowed woman who gave her all, trusting that God would care for her.

Ponder

Who do you think of as someone in your community who serves God quietly and sacrifically, as this woman did, with no thought of gaining power or influence?

Respond

Loving Jesus,
I read this story of the widow
and her wholehearted giving,
and I want to know what happened next.
How did she stay warm that night?
Who gave her food the next day?
I have to trust that your steadfast love
met her and warmed her and fed her
as you called others to be your hands
reaching out to her.
And just as you cared for her,
I can trust that you care for me too.

For the Lord is good;
his steadfast love endures forever
and his faithfulness to all generations. (Psalm 100:5)

WEEK 5
Watch & Listen to the Sustaining Jesus

Reading: Mark 13 and 14

Prayer

Restore to me the joy of your salvation,
and sustain in me a willing spirit. (Psalm 51:12)
Restore to me the joy of Your salvation
and sustain me with a willing spirit. (AMP)
Bring me back from gray exile,
put a fresh wind in my sails! (MSG)
Restore to me the joy of your salvation,
and make me willing to obey you. (NLT)
Give me the joy of your saving help again
and sustain me with your bountiful spirit. (BCP)

Define

sustain: to support, hold, or bear up from below; bear the weight of, to keep (a person, the mind, the spirits, etc.) from giving way, as under trial or affliction.[1]

Day 22: Mark 13:1-23

Restore to me the joy of your salvation, and sustain in me a willing spirit. (Psalm 51:12)

As he walked away from the Temple, one of his disciples said, "Teacher, look at that stonework! Those buildings!"

Jesus said, "You're impressed by this grandiose architecture? There's not a stone in the whole works that is not going to end up in a heap of rubble."

Later, as he was sitting on Mount Olives in full view of the Temple, Peter, James, John, and Andrew got him off by himself and asked, "Tell us, when is this going to happen? What sign will we get that things are coming to a head?"

Jesus began, "Watch out for doomsday deceivers. Many leaders are going to show up with forged identities claiming, 'I'm the One.' They will deceive a lot of people. When you hear of wars and rumored wars, keep your head and don't panic. This is routine history, and no sign of the end. Nation will fight nation and ruler fight ruler, over and over. Earthquakes will occur in various places. There will be famines. But these things are nothing compared to what's coming.

"And watch out! They're going to drag you into court. And then it will go from bad to worse, dog-eat-dog, everyone at your throat because you carry my name. You're placed there as sentinels to truth. The Message has to be preached all across the world.

"When they bring you, betrayed, into court, don't worry about what you'll say. When the time comes, say what's on your heart—the Holy Spirit will make his witness in and through you.

"It's going to be brother killing brother, father killing child, children killing parents. There's no telling who will hate you because of me.

"Stay with it—that's what is required. Stay with it to the end. You won't be sorry; you'll be saved.

"But be ready to run for it when you see the monster of desecration set up where it should never be. You who can read, make sure you understand what I'm talking about. If you're living in Judea at the time, run for the hills; if you're working in the yard, don't go back to the house to get anything; if you're out in the field, don't go back to get your coat. Pregnant and nursing

mothers will have it especially hard. Hope and pray this won't happen in the middle of winter.

"These are going to be hard days—nothing like it from the time God made the world right up to the present. And there'll be nothing like it again. If he let the days of trouble run their course, nobody would make it. But because of God's chosen people, those he personally chose, he has already intervened.

"If anyone tries to flag you down, calling out, 'Here's the Messiah!' or points, 'There he is!' don't fall for it. Fake Messiahs and lying preachers are going to pop up everywhere. Their impressive credentials and bewitching performances will pull the wool over the eyes of even those who ought to know better. So watch out. I've given you fair warning. (MSG)

Observe

Jesus warned his disciples that the future would bring terrible events: wars, earthquakes, famines and persecutions. In this study, I am focusing on watching and listening to Jesus– not the theology of end times.

Jesus encouraged his followers to remain vigilant and attentive, advising them against jumping to conclusions about every new piece of information. This is good advice for all of us.

As I read Jesus' words, I was reminded of this passage:

For the grace of God has appeared,
bringing salvation to all,
training us to renounce impiety and worldly passions
and in the present age to live
lives that are self-controlled, upright, and godly,
while we wait for the blessed hope
and the manifestation of the glory
of our great God and Savior, Jesus Christ.
He it is who gave himself for us
that he might redeem us
from all iniquity and purify for himself
a people of his own who are zealous for good deeds.
(Titus 2:11-14)

For the grace of God has been revealed,
bringing salvation to all people.
And we are instructed to turn
from godless living and sinful pleasures.
We should live in this evil world with wisdom,
righteousness, and devotion to God,
while we look forward with hope to that wonderful day
when the glory of our great God and Savior,
Jesus Christ, will be revealed.
He gave his life to free us from every kind of sin,
to cleanse us, and to make us his very own people,
totally committed to doing good deeds. (Titus 2:11-14 NLT)

Ponder

Look back at the Scriptures from Titus 2. Choose a phrase or two to use in a prayer.

Respond

Sustaining Jesus,
Help me to be aware of the events around me
without wallowing in tragedy and gloom.
Don't let me miss the small daily joys around me,
the gifts of your bountiful spirit.
Help me to live
a life that is self-controlled, upright, and godly,
while I await a glorious eternity with you.

Cast your burden on the Lord [release it]
and He will sustain and uphold you;
(Psalm 55:22 AMP)

Day 23: Mark 13:24-14:9

Restore to me the joy of your salvation,
and sustain in me a willing spirit. (Psalm 51:12)

"At that time, after the anguish of those days, the sun will be darkened, the moon will give no light, the stars will fall from the sky, and the powers in the heavens will be shaken.

Then everyone will see the Son of Man coming on the clouds with great power and glory. And he will send out his angels to gather his chosen ones from all over the world—from the farthest ends of the earth and heaven.

"Now learn a lesson from the fig tree. When its branches bud and its leaves begin to sprout, you know that summer is near. In the same way, when you see all these things taking place, you can know that his return is very near, right at the door. I tell you the truth, this generation will not pass from the scene before all these things take place. Heaven and earth will disappear, but my words will never disappear.

"However, no one knows the day or hour when these things will happen, not even the angels in heaven or the Son himself. Only the Father knows. And since you don't know when that time will come, be on guard! Stay alert!

"The coming of the Son of Man can be illustrated by the story of a man going on a long trip. When he left home, he gave each of his slaves instructions about the work they were to do, and he told the gatekeeper to watch for his return. You, too, must keep watch! For you don't know when the master of the household will return—in the evening, at midnight, before dawn, or at daybreak. Don't let him find you sleeping when he arrives without warning. I say to you what I say to everyone: Watch for him!"

It was now two days before Passover and the Festival of Unleavened Bread. The leading priests and the teachers of

religious law were still looking for an opportunity to capture Jesus secretly and kill him. "But not during the Passover celebration," they agreed, "or the people may riot."

Meanwhile, Jesus was in Bethany at the home of Simon, a man who had previously had leprosy. While he was eating, a woman came in with a beautiful alabaster jar of expensive perfume made from essence of nard. She broke open the jar and poured the perfume over his head.

Some of those at the table were indignant. "Why waste such expensive perfume?" they asked. "It could have been sold for a year's wages and the money given to the poor!" So they scolded her harshly.

But Jesus replied, "Leave her alone. Why criticize her for doing such a good thing to me? You will always have the poor among you, and you can help them whenever you want to. But you will not always have me.

She has done what she could and has anointed my body for burial ahead of time. I tell you the truth, wherever the Good News is preached throughout the world, this woman's deed will be remembered and discussed." (NLT)

Define

essence of nard: This costly perfume, worth about a year's wages for the working class, was imported from India in alabaster containers. It could have been part of the woman's dowry.

Observe

"Watch for him!" Although various branches of the Christian faith differ in their teachings about Jesus' return, we all agree that he is spiritually present with us now, gathering us into his arms and sustaining us through good times and bad.

In the Gospel of John, we learn that the woman who anointed Jesus was Mary of Bethany, whose brother Lazarus had been raised from the dead. (John 12:1-7)

I love the phrase that Jesus speaks about her: "She has done what she could." What a beautiful way to be described and remembered. It is also an encouragement to avoid comparing ourselves with others or criticizing the ways that others worship God.

Ponder

How might you choose to intentionally watch for the presence of Jesus today?

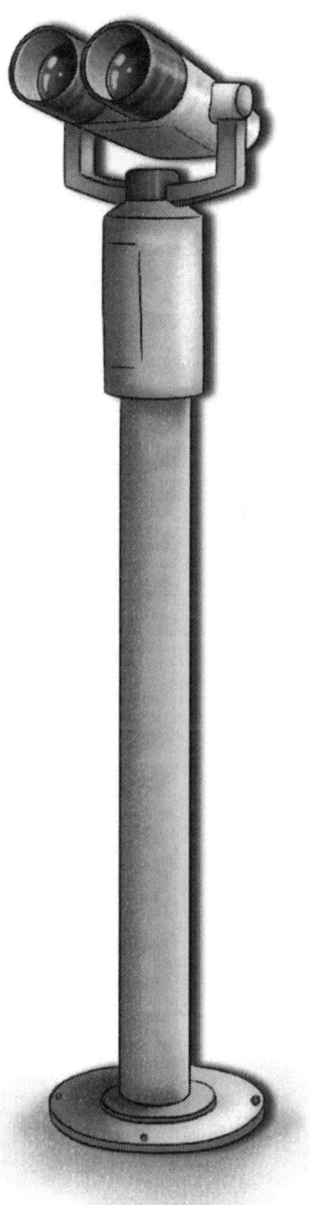

Mary gave an extravagant gift to Jesus, and she faced criticism for doing so. If you were placing this event in modern times, what do you think Mary might give Jesus?

How would you describe Jesus in today's readings? What are his character qualities and attitudes?

How does Jesus interact with people in this passage?

How would you summarize Jesus' message, in words and actions, in this passage?

Respond

Sustaining Jesus,
I think I caught a glimpse of you today
in the sunlight streaming through the trees.
I know I tasted your goodness
in a steaming bowl of fragrant soup.
I felt your reassurance deep within my soul
as I read an email that gave me a sense of hope.
I heard your voice in the Scripture,
reminding me that you are always with me.

> *...Be sure of this:*
> *I am with you always,*
> *even to the end of the age. (Matthew 28:20 NLT)*

Day 24: Mark 14:10-25

***Restore to me the joy of your salvation,
and sustain in me a willing spirit. (Psalm 51:12)***

Then Judas Iscariot, who was one of the twelve, went to the chief priests in order to betray him to them. When they heard it, they were greatly pleased and promised to give him money. So he began to look for an opportunity to betray him.

On the first day of Unleavened Bread, when the Passover lamb is sacrificed, his disciples said to him, "Where do you want us to go and make the preparations for you to eat the Passover?"

So he sent two of his disciples, saying to them, "Go into the city, and a man carrying a jar of water will meet you; follow him, and wherever he enters, say to the owner of the house, 'The Teacher asks: Where is my guest room where I may eat the Passover with my disciples?' He will show you a large room upstairs, furnished and ready. Make preparations for us there." So the disciples set out and went to the city and found everything as he had told them, and they prepared the Passover meal.

When it was evening, he came with the twelve. And when they had taken their places and were eating, Jesus said, "Truly I tell you, one of you will betray me, one who is eating with me."

They began to be distressed and to say to him one after another, "Surely, not I?"

He said to them, "It is one of the twelve, one who is dipping bread into the bowl with me. For the Son of Man goes as it is written of him, but woe to that one by whom the Son of Man is betrayed! It would have been better for that one not to have been born."

While they were eating, he took a loaf of bread, and after blessing it he broke it, gave it to them, and said, "Take; this is my body."

Then he took a cup, and after giving thanks he gave it to them, and all of them drank from it. He said to them, "This is my blood of the covenant, which is poured out for many. Truly I tell you, I will never again drink of the fruit of the vine until that day when I drink it new in the kingdom of God."

Define

a large room upstairs: In the book of Acts, we read that the early church met in a home owned by Mary, the mother of John Mark. It is very possible that the room mentioned here is in that same home. And if so, Mark the Gospel Author probably had a personal memory of this event.

Observe

In the middle of a commemorative meal, as they remembered God's rescue of their ancestors, Jesus introduced a new commemoration. This is a meal for all us, in remembrance of our savior and rescuer, Jesus Christ.

Ponder

What do you think the disciples might have been feeling during this meal? Jesus interrupted their yearly festive meal with comments about someone betraying him. Each of them questioned whether they might be that betrayer. Then Jesus spoke the words about his body and his blood. These words that have become so familiar to us must have sounded cryptic to the disciples.

Respond

Sustaining Jesus,

You gave us the cup of salvation

to sustain and nourish us

before you drank the cup of suffering

on our behalf.

> *Behold, God is my helper and ally;*
> *The Lord is the sustainer of my soul [my upholder].*
> *(Psalm 54:4 AMP)*

Day 25: Mark 14:22-42

Restore to me the joy of your salvation, and sustain in me a willing spirit. (Psalm 51:12)

When they had sung the hymn, they went out to the Mount of Olives. And Jesus said to them, "You will all fall away, for it is written, 'I will strike the shepherd, and the sheep will be scattered.'

"But after I am raised up, I will go before you to Galilee."

Peter said to him, "Even though all fall away, I will not."

Jesus said to him, "Truly I tell you, this day, this very night, before the cock crows twice, you will deny me three times."

But he said vehemently, "Even though I must die with you, I will not deny you." And all of them said the same.

They went to a place called Gethsemane, and he said to his disciples, "Sit here while I pray." He took with him Peter and James and John and began to be distressed and agitated. And he said to them, "My soul is deeply grieved, even to death; remain here, and keep awake." And going a little farther, he threw himself on the ground and prayed that, if it were possible, the hour might pass from him. He said, "Abba, Father, for you all things are possible; remove this cup from me, yet not what I want but what you want."

He came and found them sleeping, and he said to Peter, "Simon, are you asleep? Could you not keep awake one hour? Keep awake and pray that you may not come into the time of trial; the spirit indeed is willing, but the flesh is weak."

And again he went away and prayed, saying the same words. And once more he came and found them sleeping, for their eyes were very heavy, and they did not know what to say to him.

He came a third time and said to them, "Are you still sleeping and taking your rest? Enough! The hour has come; the Son of Man is betrayed into the hands of sinners. Get up, let us be going. Look, my betrayer is at hand."

Define

when they had sung the hymn: Passover celebrations ended with the singing of Psalm 118.[2]

Observe

Out of my distress I called on the Lord;
the Lord answered me and set me in a broad place.
With the Lord on my side I do not fear.
What can mortals do to me?...
O give thanks to the Lord, for he is good,
for his steadfast love endures forever. (Psalm 118:5-6, 29)

With the words of Psalm 118 echoing in their minds, the sleepy disciples headed to a garden with their Rabbi. Jesus knew what awaited him. He knew that the sacrificial lamb of the Passover was an illustration of the sacrifice he would soon become. The garden must have been a familiar location, because Judas was able to predict that Jesus would be there.

In the first chapter of Mark, we read God the Father's words to his beloved son. In today's passage we read Jesus' passionate prayer to his Father, his *Abba*. It is always touching to realize that *Abba* is an "infant's intimate name for the father."[3]

Ponder

How would you describe Jesus' character and emotions in this passage?

Respond

Sustaining Jesus,

The readings are becoming more difficult now.

I want to rush past the treachery, agony, and death.

I want to turn the pages quickly,

to reach Easter Sunday as soon as possible.

But life doesn't work that way.

You had to endure one day and one night at a time,

and you will sustain me as I live this day.

> *Lord, sustain me as you promised, that I may live!*
> *Do not let my hope be crushed.*
> *Sustain me, and I will be rescued;*
> *then I will meditate continually on your decrees.*
> *(Psalm 119:116-117 NLT)*

Day 26: Mark 14:43-72

***Restore to me the joy of your salvation,
and sustain in me a willing spirit. (Psalm 51:12)***

Immediately, while he was still speaking, Judas, one of the twelve, arrived, and with him there was a crowd with swords and clubs, from the chief priests, the scribes, and the elders. Now the betrayer had given them a sign, saying, "The one I will kiss is the man; arrest him and lead him away under guard." So when he came, he went up to him at once and said, "Rabbi!" and kissed him. Then they laid hands on him and arrested him.

But one of those who stood near drew his sword and struck the slave of the high priest, cutting off his ear. Then Jesus said to them, "Have you come out with swords and clubs to arrest me as though I were a rebel? Day after day I was with you in the temple teaching, and you did not arrest me. But let the scriptures be fulfilled." All of them [the disciples] deserted him and fled.

A certain young man was following him, wearing nothing but a linen cloth. They caught hold of him, but he left the linen cloth and ran off naked.

They took Jesus to the high priest, and all the chief priests, the elders, and the scribes were assembled. Peter had followed him at a distance, right into the courtyard of the high priest, and he was sitting with the guards, warming himself at the fire.

Now the chief priests and the whole council were looking for testimony against Jesus to put him to death, but they found none. For many gave false testimony against him, and their testimony did not agree. Some stood up and gave false testimony against him, saying, "We heard him say, 'I will destroy this temple that is made with hands, and in three days I will build another, not made with hands.' " But even on this point their testimony did not agree.

Then the high priest stood up before them and asked Jesus, "Have you no answer? What is it that they testify against you?" But he was silent and did not answer. Again the high priest asked him, "Are you the Messiah, the Son of the Blessed One?"

Jesus said, "I am, and 'you will see the Son of Man seated at the right hand of the Power' and 'coming with the clouds of heaven.' "

Then the high priest tore his clothes and said, "Why do we still need witnesses? You have heard his blasphemy! What is your decision?"

All of them condemned him as deserving death. Some began to spit on him, to blindfold him, and to strike him, saying to him, "Prophesy!" The guards also took him and beat him.

While Peter was below in the courtyard, one of the female servants of the high priest came by. When she saw Peter warming himself, she stared at him and said, "You also were with Jesus, the man from Nazareth."

But he denied it, saying, "I do not know or understand what you are talking about." And he went out into the forecourt. Then the cock crowed.

And the female servant, on seeing him, began again to say to the bystanders, "This man is one of them." But again he denied it.

Then after a little while the bystanders again said to Peter, "Certainly you are one of them, for you are a Galilean, and you talk like one."

But he began to curse, and he swore an oath, "I do not know this man you are talking about." At that moment the cock crowed for the second time.

Then Peter remembered that Jesus had said to him, "Before the cock crows twice, you will deny me three times." And he broke down and wept.

Define

a certain young man: Because this person is only mentioned in the book of Mark, many scholars believe that it is Mark himself.

Observe

It is interesting to speculate what it might have been like for the young John Mark to experience the Passover dinner in his home with Jesus and his disciples. Did he nod off after the holiday meal? Was he wakened by the "crowd with clubs and swords" on their way to arrest Jesus? Did he grab a cloth to wrap around himself so he could dash off to the garden–only to find himself too late to warn the Rabbi Jesus? If so, what a sense of failure and helplessness he must have felt!

This reading is full of failure: Judas, Peter, and the false witnesses. I'm sure that the disciples were thinking that Jesus had failed. Where was their mightly rescuing Messiah?

But Jesus, mocked and beaten and wrongly accused, knew that glory awaited. Jesus endured.

Ponder

How would you describe Jesus in this reading? What are his character qualities?

Respond

Lord Jesus,
when I fail
when I want to give up
remind me that you
who endured the unimaginable
are right beside me
sustaining me.

...Let us run with endurance the race God has set before us.
We do this by keeping our eyes on Jesus,
the champion who initiates and perfects our faith.
Because of the joy awaiting him, he endured the cross,
disregarding its shame.
Now he is seated in the place of honor
beside God's throne.
Think of all the hostility he endured from sinful people;
then you won't become weary and give up.
(Hebrews 12:1-3 NLT)

WEEK 6
Watch & Listen to the Enlightening Jesus

Reading: Mark 15-16

Prayer

The Lord is God,
and he has given us light... (Psalm 118:27)
The Lord is God, and He has given us light
[illuminating us with His grace and freedom and joy]... (AMP)
God is God, he has bathed us in light. (MSG)
The Lord is God, shining upon us... (NLT)
God is the Lord, he has shined upon us... (BCP)

Day 27: Mark 15:1-15

The Lord is God, and he has given us light... (Psalm 118:27)

At dawn's first light, the high priests, with the religious leaders and scholars, arranged a conference with the entire Jewish Council. After tying Jesus securely, they took him out and presented him to Pilate.

Pilate asked him, "Are you the 'King of the Jews'?"

He answered, "If you say so." The high priests let loose a barrage of accusations.

Pilate asked again, "Aren't you going to answer anything? That's quite a list of accusations." Still, he said nothing. Pilate was impressed, really impressed.

It was a custom at the Feast to release a prisoner, anyone the people asked for. There was one prisoner called Barabbas, locked up with the insurrectionists who had committed murder during the uprising against Rome. As the crowd came up and began to present its petition for him to release a prisoner, Pilate anticipated them: "Do you want me to release the King of the Jews to you?" Pilate knew by this time that it was through sheer spite that the high priests had turned Jesus over to him.

But the high priests by then had worked up the crowd to ask for the release of Barabbas. Pilate came back, "So what do I do with this man you call King of the Jews?"

They yelled, "Nail him to a cross!"

Pilate objected, "But for what crime?"

But they yelled all the louder, "Nail him to a cross!"

Pilate gave the crowd what it wanted, set Barabbas free and turned Jesus over for whipping and crucifixion. (MSG)

Define

Barabbas: this Jewish man belonged to a political group that was using violence in an attempt to overthrow the Roman government.[1]

Observe

From the beginning of Mark's gospel, we have seen how the religious leaders felt threatened by Jesus, and how they constantly plotted to get rid of him. Now they brought Jesus to Pilate, a government official that Rome had placed in power over all of them. Although these religious leaders longed for the Roman officials to be overthrown, they were not above using them for their own purposes.

Pilate knew his own power was threatened by a "King of the Jews," so he had to take action. The scene seems to be out of control, a downhill slide of events leading one to another as the leaders influence the mob to do their will.

But Jesus has always seen this coming.

Ponder

Why do you think the crowds moved so quickly from praising Jesus as he entered Jerusalem (on what we call Palm Sunday) to begging for his crucifixion a few days later?

Respond

Enlightening Jesus,

You who spoke the world into existence

said only a few words

as the powers of darkness endeavored to put out your light.

The Light shines on in the darkness,
and the darkness did not understand it
or overpower it
or appropriate it
or absorb it
[and is unreceptive to it]. (John 1:5 AMP)

Day 28: Mark 15:16-25

The Lord is God, and he has given us light...
(Psalm 118:27)

The soldiers led Him away into the palace (that is, the Praetorium), and they called together the entire [Roman] battalion [of 600 soldiers]. They dressed Him up in [a ranking Roman officer's robe of] purple, and after twisting [together] a crown of thorns, they placed it on Him; and they began saluting and mocking Him: "Hail, King of the Jews!" They kept beating Him on the head with a reed and spitting on Him, and kneeling and bowing in [mock] homage to Him. After they had mocked Him, they took off the purple robe and put His own clothes on Him. And they led Him out [of the city] to crucify Him.

They forced into service a passer-by coming in from the countryside, Simon of Cyrene (the father of Alexander and Rufus), to carry His cross.

Then they brought Him to the place [called] Golgotha, which is translated, Place of a Skull. They tried to give Him wine mixed with myrrh [to dull the pain], but He would not take it. And they crucified Him, and divided up His clothes among themselves, casting lots for them to see who should take what. It was the third hour (9:00 a.m.) when they crucified Him.
(AMP)

Define

Simon of Cyrene (the father of Alexander and Rufus): Cyrene was a city in North Africa (modern day Libya) which included a large Jewish community. Simon had probably traveled to Jerusalem for the Passover. Mark may have listed Simon's sons because his readers knew them; the Apostle Paul mentioned a man named Rufus in Romans 16:3.

Observe

Just a few days before, Jesus told a parable about a vineyard whose tenants attacked the messengers who were sent by the landlord (Mark 12:1-12). In this story, the Landlord decided to send one more messenger–his son. Surely they will respect his son! But the tenants wanted to continue their control over the vineyard, so they killed the son.

Now this parable has come to life, with the earthly powers killing the heavenly messenger, the Son, the Beloved.

Ponder

Within his description of the Crucifixion, Mark gives us a few words about a man named Simon who was compelled by the Romans to carry Jesus' cross. Take a few moments to imagine what this might have been like for Simon.

Respond

Enlightening Jesus,

On that dark day they crowned you with thorns

and knelt before you in mockery

and you –the Almighty–

were too weak to carry your cross

while you shouldered all our sorrows

and carried all our griefs.

He was despised and rejected by others;
a man of suffering and acquainted with infirmity,
and as one from whom others hide their faces
he was despised, and we held him of no account.
Surely he has borne our infirmities
and carried our diseases,
yet we accounted him stricken,
struck down by God, and afflicted.
But he was wounded for our transgressions,
crushed for our iniquities;
upon him was the punishment that made us whole,
and by his bruises we are healed. (Isaiah 53:3-5)

Day 29: Mark 15:26-39

The Lord is God, and he has given us light... (Psalm 118:27)

The inscription of the accusation against Him had been written [above Him]: "THE KING OF THE JEWS." They crucified two robbers with Him, one on His right and one on His left. [And the Scripture was fulfilled which says, "He was counted with the transgressors."]

Those who were passing by were insulting Him with abusive and insolent language, wagging their heads [as a sign of contempt], and saying, "Ha! You who would destroy the temple and rebuild it in [only] three days, save Yourself by coming down from the cross!"

In the same way the chief priests also, along with the scribes, were ridiculing and mocking Him among themselves and saying, "He saved others [from death]; He cannot save Himself! Let the Christ (the Messiah, the Anointed), the King of Israel, now come down from the cross, so that we may see and believe and trust [in Him]!" Those who were crucified with Him were also insulting Him.

When the sixth hour (noon) came, darkness covered the whole land until the ninth hour (3:00 p.m.). And at the ninth hour Jesus cried out with a loud voice, "Eloi, Eloi, lama sabachthani?"—which is translated, "My God, My God, why have You forsaken Me?"

Some of the bystanders heard Him and said, "Look! He is calling for Elijah!" Someone ran and filled a sponge with sour wine, put it on a reed and gave Him a drink, saying, "Let us see whether Elijah is coming to take Him down."

But Jesus uttered a loud cry, and breathed out His last [voluntarily, sovereignly dismissing and releasing His spirit from His body in submission to His Father's plan].

And the veil [of the Holy of Holies] of the temple was torn in two from top to bottom.

When the centurion, who was standing opposite Him, saw the way He breathed His last [being fully in control], he said, "Truly this man was the Son of God!" (AMP)

Define

My God, My God, why have You forsaken Me?: This is a quote from Psalm 22:1.

Observe

In the first chapter of Mark, we heard the Father's words, introducing us to his beloved Son. Now in Mark 15, we hear a Roman commander, an expert in torture and execution, coming to the profound realization that this was no mere man, this was the Son of God on the cross.

The Romans referred to their emperor as a "Son of God," so this was indeed a shocking statement for him to make.

I remember watching an Easter pageant several years ago. It seemed odd to me when the Roman soldiers joined the disciples for a final song. And then I realized there was nothing incongruous about it. At the foot of the cross, we are all equal, and we are all welcome.

Ponder

Here are a few more verses from Psalm 22. It is interesting to consider what they meant to Jesus during this desperate time.

My God, my God, why have you forsaken me?
Why are you so far from helping me,
from the words of my groaning?
O my God, I cry by day, but you do not answer;
and by night but find no rest.
Yet you are holy,
enthroned on the praises of Israel.
In you our ancestors trusted;
they trusted, and you delivered them.
To you they cried and were saved;
in you they trusted and were not put to shame.
But I am a worm and not human,
scorned by others and despised by the people.
All who see me mock me;
they sneer at me; they shake their heads;

"Commit your cause to the Lord; let him deliver—
let him rescue the one in whom he delights!"
...Do not be far from me,
for trouble is near,
and there is no one to help. (Psalm 22:1-8, 11)

Respond

The Light of the World breathed his last.

But it wasn't the end

it was the beginning

the dawn of a new day

in which there is no curtain between us and you, Lord,

and we are all equal before you.

Day 30: Mark 15:40-47

The Lord is God, and he has given us light... (Psalm 118:27)

Now some women also were watching from a distance, among whom were Mary Magdalene, and Mary the mother of James the Less and of Joses, and Salome. When Jesus was in Galilee, they used to accompany him and minister to Him; and there were also many other women who came up with Him to Jerusalem.

When evening had already come, because it was the preparation day, that is, the day before the Sabbath, Joseph of Arimathea came, a prominent and respected member of the Council (Sanhedrin, Jewish High Court), who was himself waiting for the kingdom of God—and he courageously dared to go in before Pilate, and asked for the body of Jesus.

Pilate wondered if He was dead by this time [only six hours after being crucified], and he summoned the centurion and asked him whether He was already dead. And when he learned from the centurion [that Jesus was in fact dead], he gave the body to Joseph [by granting him permission to remove it].

So Joseph purchased a [fine] linen cloth [for wrapping the body], and after taking Jesus down [from the cross], he wrapped Him in the linen cloth and placed Him in a tomb which had been cut out of rock. Then he rolled a [large, wheel-shaped] stone against the entrance of the tomb.

Mary Magdalene and Mary the mother of Joses were [carefully] watching to see where He was laid. (AMP)

Define

some women: the group of women includes two mothers of disciples: Mary, the mother of James the Less, and his brother Joses (not a disciple), and Salome, the mother of James and John. Salome is believed to be one of the sisters of Jesus' mother, Mary.[2]

Observe

Joseph of Arimathea was a wealthy and influential member of the Jewish council as well as a secret follower of Jesus.

(John 19:38) Joseph demonstrated great courage when he approached Pontius Pilate to request Jesus' body. After preparing it for burial, he placed the body in a newly constructed tomb in a garden.

The women displayed their own quiet, determined courage as they waited to see where Jesus was buried so that they could do what they thought would be one last service for him.

Ponder

If you were in an Easter Pageant, which character would you want to play in this scene? What emotions would you aim to convey through your portrayal?

- Joseph of Arimathea
- the Centurion
- Simon of Cyrene
- one of the women

Respond

All hope was lost.
Yet somehow the women
and Joseph
kept putting one foot in front of the other
doing the things that needed to be done.
Thank you, Jesus,
for these portraits in courage,
and thank you that
contrary to what seemed to have happened
hope was not lost.

Let your unfailing love surround us,
Lord, for our hope is in you alone. (Psalm 33:22)

Day 31: Mark 16

The Lord is God, and he has given us light... (Psalm 118:27)

The Gospel of Mark was the first Gospel to be written, and ancient copies give us three different endings of it. I call them the Abrupt Ending, the Short Ending, and the Longer Ending. It is easy to picture a scribe copying the Gospel at some point in the early church era, and deciding to add just a few more details.

On Saturday evening, when the Sabbath ended, Mary Magdalene, Mary the mother of James, and Salome went out and purchased burial spices so they could anoint Jesus' body. Very early on Sunday morning, just at sunrise, they went to the tomb. On the way they were asking each other, "Who will roll away the stone for us from the entrance to the tomb?" But as they arrived, they looked up and saw that the stone, which was very large, had already been rolled aside.

When they entered the tomb, they saw a young man clothed in a white robe sitting on the right side. The women were shocked, but the angel said, "Don't be alarmed. You are looking for Jesus of Nazareth, who was crucified. He isn't here! He is risen from the dead! Look, this is where they laid his body. Now go and tell his disciples, including Peter, that Jesus is going ahead of you to Galilee. You will see him there, just as he told you before he died." The women fled from the tomb, trembling and bewildered, and they said nothing to anyone because they were too frightened. **[Abrupt ending]**

Then they briefly reported all this to Peter and his companions. Afterward Jesus himself sent them out from east to west with the sacred and unfailing message of salvation that gives eternal life. Amen. **[Short ending]**

After Jesus rose from the dead early on Sunday morning, the first person who saw him was Mary Magdalene, the woman from whom he had cast out seven demons. She went to the disciples, who were grieving and weeping, and told them what had happened. But when she told them that Jesus was alive and she had seen him, they didn't believe her.

Afterward he appeared in a different form to two of his followers who were walking from Jerusalem into the country. They rushed back to tell the others, but no one believed them. Still later he appeared to the eleven disciples as they were eating together. He rebuked them for their stubborn unbelief because they refused to believe those who had seen him after he had been raised from the dead.

And then he told them, "Go into all the world and preach the Good News to everyone. Anyone who believes and is baptized will be saved. But anyone who refuses to believe will be condemned. These miraculous signs will accompany those who believe: They will cast out demons in my name, and they will speak in new languages. They will be able to handle snakes with safety, and if they drink anything poisonous, it won't hurt them. They will be able to place their hands on the sick, and they will be healed."

When the Lord Jesus had finished talking with them, he was taken up into heaven and sat down in the place of honor at God's right hand. And the disciples went everywhere and preached, and the Lord worked through them, confirming what they said by many miraculous signs. **[Long Ending, not included in the oldest existing copies]** *(NLT)*

Observe

Many of the details of the long ending could be gleaned from the other Gospels. The words about snakes and poisons seem a bit fanciful, leading me to agree with the idea that this long ending was added at some point. In fact, it does not exist in the oldest copies of Mark.

I think that both the abrupt ending and the short ending are very much in Mark's brief style of writing. He gives us the basic details and the amazing news of the Resurrection, and then he stops. This is the Good News. What else do you need to know?

The abruptness of it reminds me of the way our church service on Palm Sunday ends, skipping any sort of dismissal. As we enter Holy Week, we are conscious that we are commemorating a series of events that unfolded one after the other, and it won't be over until Easter Morning. On this journey, we remember the joy of the Triumphal Entry, the fellowship of the Last Supper, and the anguish in the Garden of Gethsemane. We remember the tragic hours of the trial and the Crucifixion, and the dark days after that when the disciples huddled together in fear and grief. But unlike them, we have the luxury of knowing that Easter Sunday awaits.

This last chapter of Mark is a beautiful passage to picture. You can imagine the women approaching the tomb at sunrise, wondering how in the world they are going to move that huge rock. You can envision their shock and surprise at meeting an angel. Then the unbelievable truth of the Resurrection begins to dawn up on them. At first they don't know what to do with this information. Surely the disciples won't believe them! But eventually they rush off to share the good news, and as they do this, they become the Apostles to the Apostles.

This sunrise scene is the reason I chose the theme of enlightenment for this chapter. Jesus is alive, and his followers now begin to understand his identity, his mission, and his life-changing call to all of us. Remember Jesus' first words in this gospel?

> *...The time is fulfilled, and the kingdom of God has come near; repent, and believe in the good news. (Mark 1:15)*
>
> *...The [appointed period of] time is fulfilled, and the kingdom of God is at hand; repent [change your inner self—your old way of thinking, regret past sins, live your life in a way that proves repentance; seek God's purpose for your life] and believe [with a deep, abiding trust] in the good news. (AMP)*

Jesus is present with us now, and he continually gives us opportunities to change and grow and to live our lives in ways

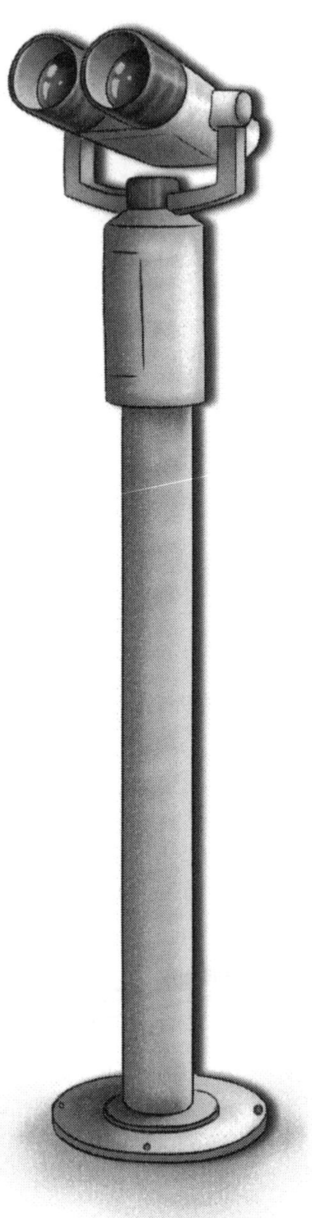

that prove repentance. As we seek his purpose for our lives, he continues to love us, sustain us, and enlighten us.

Ponder

What have you observed in this study about the power of Jesus to change lives?

How does this encourage you?

Read the prayer on the next page, noticing the descriptions of Jesus which have been our chapter titles. Which of them is most meaningful to you today?

Respond

Teaching Jesus,

I am watching and listening to you, asking for your guidance.

Listening Jesus,

you hear my every word and you understand my heart.

Reviving Jesus,

you are my source of hope and renewal in every season of life.

Steadfastly Loving Jesus,

I depend on your constant love to encourage and nourish me,

enabling me to share this love with others.

Sustaining Jesus,

I am comforted to know that you uphold and support me every day.

Enlightening Jesus,

you open your truth to me and reveal the way forward.

The mighty one, God the Lord, speaks. (Psalm 50:1a)
Make me to know your ways, O Lord;
teach me your paths. (Psalm 25:4)
For he did not despise or abhor the affliction of the afflicted;
He did not hide his face from me,
but heard when I cried to him. (Psalm 22:24)
The law of the Lord is perfect,
reviving the soul. (Psalm 19:7)
Let them thank the Lord for his steadfast love,
for his wonderful works to humankind. (Psalm 107:21)
Restore to me the joy of your salvation,
and sustain in me a willing spirit. (Psalm 51:12)
The Lord is God,
and he has given us light… (Psalm 118:27)

APPENDIX

Footnotes

Introduction

1. Online concordance at https://www.blueletterbible.org/lexicon/g5547/kjv/tr/0-1/, accessed November 1, 2023
2. Card, Michael, *Mark: The Gospel of Passion* (Downer's Grove, Illinois: Intervarsity Press, 2012), p. 27
3. Ibid., p. 35
4. Online concordance at https://www.blueletterbible.org/lexicon/g3340/kjv/tr/0-1/, accessed November 1, 2023
5. Kent, Keri Wyatt, *99 Bible Words You Should Know* (Hoffman Estates, IL: A Powerful Story, 2014), p. 160
6. I Peter 5:13
7. Colossians 4:10, 2 Timothy 4:11
8. These verses are taken from the Psalms read during Sundays in Lent in Year B, according to the Revised Common Lectionary

Chapter 1

1. Footnote in the *Amplified Study Bible*, online resource at biblegateway.com, accessed November 1, 2023

Chapter 2

1. Card, Michael, *Mark: The Gospel of Passion* (Downer's Grove, Illinois: Intervarsity Press, 2012), p. 65

Chapter 3

1. Online resource at https://www.dictionary.com/browse/revive, accessed November 1, 2023
2. Footnote in the *Amplified Study Bible*, online resource at biblegateway.com, accessed November 1, 2023

Chapter 4

1. Online resources at https://www.blueletterbible.org/lexicon/h2617/kjv/wlc/0-1/, accessed November 1, 2023
2. Footnote in the *Amplified Study Bible*, online resource at biblegateway.com, accessed November 1, 2023
3. Wright, N. T., *Mark for Everyone* (London, UK: Society for Promoting Christian Knowledge, 2004), p. 151

Chapter 5

1. summarized from online resource: https://www.dictionary.com/browse/sustain, accessed November 1, 2023
2. Online resource: https://www.crossway.org/articles/when-jesus-sang/, accessed November 1, 2023
3. Card, Michael, *Mark: The Gospel of Passion* (Downer's Grove, Illinois: Intervarsity Press, 2012), p. 170.

Chapter 6

1. Wright, N. T., *Mark for Everyone* (London, UK: Society for Promoting Christian Knowledge, 2004), p. 209
2. Footnote in the *Amplified Study Bible*, online resource at biblegateway.com, accessed November 1, 2023

Using this Book in a Group

When I lead a Bible study, it is important to me that the members do not feel stressed if they are unable to complete the assigned readings every week. Although I hope and pray that class members will make a commitment to the Lord to read the material, I understand this is a personal commitment and life will bring interruptions to each of us.

With this in mind, I have chosen one daily segment each week to focus on in class. When the class begins, we will all open our books and read that one daily segment together, and then we will discuss it. This allows everyone (those who have read at home, those who haven't, and any newcomers) to be on the same page, reading the same Scriptures together and discussing what they just read.

After that, if there is time, I will ask the class what they gleaned from any personal readings at home.

Here are the daily segments on which to focus during group discussions.

Intro week: Day 1, page 4
Week 1: Day 3, page 17
Week 2: Day 9, page 41
Week 3: Day 15, page 69
Week 4: Day 18, page 83
Week 5: Day 23, page 105

Week 6: Day 31, page 135 (If you are using this book during Lent, and ending on Palm Sunday, you may want to discuss Day 19.)this time.)

Using this Book during Lent

To use this book as a Lenten study, begin the week before (or the Sunday before) Ash Wednesday, and if you are in a group, meet together to read the Introduction.

Read Week 1 at your first meeting after Ash Wednesday, and then continue to read a week of readings (a chapter) each week. You will finish the book on the week of Palm Sunday.

I labeled the chapters so that if you are discussing them on Sundays, you discuss Week 1 on the First Sunday of Lent, Week 2 on the Second Sunday of Lent, and so on.

Made in the USA
Columbia, SC
11 January 2024